step up

How to build your influence at work

MICHELLE GIBBINGS

Published by Major Street Publishing
www.majorstreet.com.au
Contact: e l info@majorstreet.com.au p l +61 421 707 983
© Michelle Therese Gibbings 2016
The moral rights of the author have been asserted

National Library of Australia Cataloguing-in-Publication entry
Creator: Gibbings, Michelle, author.
Title: Step up : how to build your influence at work / Michelle Gibbings.
ISBN: 9780994256058 (paperback)
Notes: Includes bibliographical references and index.
Subjects: Organizational change.
                Success in business
                Development leadership.
Dewey Number: 658.406

All rights reserved. Except as permitted under the *Australian Copyright Act 1968* (for example, a fair dealing for the purposes of study, research, criticism or review), no part of this book may be reproduced, stored in a retrieval system, communicated or transmitted in any form or by any means without prior written permission. All inquiries should be made to the publisher.

Internal design by Production Works
Cover design by Ralph Cavero
Printed in Australia by
10 9 8 7 6 5 4 3 2 1

DISCLAIMER

The material in this publication is of the nature of general comment only, and does not represent professional advice. It is not intended to provide specific guidance for particular circumstances and it should not be relied on as the basis for any decision to take action or not take action on any matter which it covers. Readers should obtain professional advice where appropriate, before making any such decision. To maximum extent permitted by law, the author and publisher disclaim all responsibility and liability to any person, arising directly or indirectly from any person taking or not taking action based upon the information in this publication.

Praise for *Step Up*

Michelle Gibbings has written an excellent book which deserves a wide audience. One of the key issues facing technical people in organisations is how to build on their skills and expertise to gain greater influence and promotion into senior positions. Michelle has written an eminently practical book which will assist many people to do just this. Her personal insights and ideas will inspire all of those who wish to advance their careers and indeed their lives.

Elizabeth Proust AO, company director and former banking executive

Michelle Gibbings' *Step Up* is a clear, accessible guide to influencing progress for self and for organisation. Reaching out to both emerging and well-established leaders, she powerfully narrates experiences and examples in shaping messages and activating transformation in complex organisations and systems. A leader in her own right, Gibbings shares her acumen and distils the character and lessons of many leaders: utilising integrity, agility, insight and impact to motivate, communicate and mobilise. *Step Up* packs a hefty punch: a book providing the opportunity for anyone, anywhere to forge ahead on tough 21st-century challenges – personal or organisational.

Richard Dent OAM, CEO of Leadership Victoria

Crucial to a successful career, and to an extent life, is the ability to influence others. Michelle Gibbings has written an easy to read and practical guide to building your influencing skills. This guide would assist people working in the private, public and non-profit sectors.

Helen Silver AO, corporate senior executive and former Secretary of the Victorian Department of Premier and Cabinet

Authentic, practical and insightful Michelle Gibbings writes about change with the authority of someone who has lived it and someone who has brought the understanding of self and organisation together in a most readable form. *Step Up* brings a deep understanding from much of what has been written on the psychology of the individual and the understanding of organisational behaviour to produce a most useful book for those wanting to leverage their technical competence so as to have impact by working with others to achieve valuable outcomes. This is a must-read for anyone in business, information technology and the public sector wishing to engage their careers in today's agile and innovative economy.

Russell Yardley, Chairman of Readify, Folk and Tesserent and Director of Wunderman-Bienalto and VGPB

If you are coming from an area of strong technical competence and looking for insight on how to have greater impact in your organisation and make your voice heard at the table, then I can recommend Michelle Gibbings' book *Step Up*. It is an excellent read which provides practical tools and techniques developed from real life experience in the corporate sector. Michelle shares many personal experiences which like me I am sure you will relate to. These stories bring the book to life and enhance the application of the tools and techniques.

Christine Bartlett, company director

Step Up is an excellent book with key tips, principles, case studies and examples critical to successfully lead in business. The guidance in this book will have a very big impact on the leadership of the reader. During my career, I have applied many of the principles in the book and they have had a profound impact on my leadership and how I bring my "whole self" to work. They've been instrumental to my career success. I'd encourage *Step Up* to anyone who wants to take their career to the next level.

Greg Braddy, Executive General Manager, Chief Financial Officer, Business Banking, NAB

Step Up provides essential guidance for aspiring and current leaders. Its use of practical steps, studies and references brings worldly wisdom to the book's approach. The reader is encouraged to make the learnings personal and relevant to their work environment through a series of self-assessments. Throughout the book, Michelle ensures the reader is challenged and inspired to think and act differently. A must read for all those looking to advance their career.

Carlo Cataldo, Chief Risk Officer, ME Bank

Step Up is an easily digestible, pragmatic and accurate roadmap aimed at building and maintaining relevance and profile within organisations of all sizes and environments. It will be appealing to leaders at all levels, but especially to those who are about to leap into unfamiliar or challenging roles or territory. Michelle does well to call out that which can and cannot be influenced, and her approach is particularly relevant to those moving from functional management to senior executive leadership roles.

Sean Hughes, Chief Risk and Legal Officer, Unisuper Management

If ever there was a time where change is accelerating at break neck pace, it is now. Consequently, the skills needed to more effectively influence and thereby better lead those around you are becoming increasingly valued by organisations.

To better meet these challenges, there is no doubt that *Step Up* will provide you will some wonderful frameworks to support you. In her own engaging style, Michelle shares some practical and easily implementable methodologies for behaviour change. This book is NOT simply another step by step guide to changing behaviour. It is a book that if read with a receptive 'learner' mindset, will bring you to a greater understanding of the value that can be created through improving your influencing skills.

Throughout the book, Michelle covers a range of subjects all designed to raise your influencing skills, each supported by a series of "check point" activities which, when properly completed, will help you to embed your learnings.

I have always been impressed by the effortless and pragmatic manner in which Michelle influences those around her. It seems only fitting then that she utilise these skills and her many years of authentic leadership in this field to share her learnings with you.

By the end of this book, you will have a much better understanding of:

- Why you need to change the way you influence in the workplace
- How you make the behavioural change needed to become a better influencer
- What you need to do to embed this change to make influencing habitual

If your aim is to step up and improve your influence at work, then I wholeheartedly recommend Michelle's book to help you gain a much better understanding of the keys skills needed to help get you there!

Tim Mitchell-Adams, Managing Director – Charter & Ipac, AMP Limited

The hierarchical organisation where leaders are at the top, and those below them simply follow is increasingly rare. Getting stuff done is about people engaging and influencing people – not only within an organisation but also across all of the partners and stakeholders that are needed to make an initiative, project or aspiration a reality. In *Step Up*, Michelle shares her deep experience and insight to this critical part of the tool kit of every effective leader."

Kate Vinot, Director, City Strategy and Place, City of Melbourne

As a long-time member of the "Cardigan Brigade" (see page 1) I have seen many technical people who have really struggled to get their point across. This easily digestible book will help subject matter experts self-reflect and provides support to empower them in how best to present, negotiate and influence positively. A highly accessible leadership book suitable for all technical team members, whatever role they are in.

Carolyn Hanson, President of the Governance Risk and Compliance Institute

Step Up is a book packed with insights and practical advice to help leaders make a difference. Michelle challenges and encourages the reader to look within themselves and then shows them how to influence with impact. A must read for anyone who takes leadership seriously.

Gabrielle Dolan, Key note speaker and author of "Ignite: Real leadership, real talk, real results"

A great mix of personal experience, practical models and theory to allow an individual to maximise their influencing skills and navigate an organisation successfully.

Carly Rees, General Manager, Global Enterprise and Services PMO & Change, Telstra

In an age when our work environments are becoming faster and more complex – and saturated with 'change' – the opportunity for technical corporate specialists to step out of their comfort zones and realise their potential has never been richer. Michelle Gibbings' book illuminates the power and potential of the insightful influencer, providing easy to understand and well tested frameworks and working examples. As a blend of science (you'll never think about your brain in the same way again!), philosophies and personal experience, it is clear that this book has been crafted by someone who is passionate about seeing the technical specialist become as important to successful, impactful and quality decision making as those who run out front and traditionally get the glory for a company's success.

Robyn Weatherley, Australian corporate governance practitioner and published author "Eyes Wide Open – A First Timer's Guide to the Real World of Boards and Company Directorship"

A rare blend of expertise, theory, and practical advice, *Step Up* is aimed at mid-career professionals in functional roles wanting to expand their influence within organisations. As challenging as it is enlightening, readers are asked to question their individual beliefs and practices, and to then reflect on themselves within an organisational context. Most importantly, I felt I was on a journey moving forward while I was reading. The way Michelle Gibbings shares personal stories and incorporates research in an easy-to-read narrative meant I felt was I gaining insights into how to be more successful at negotiating and managing my professional career. This book is a valuable addition to any professional library.

Dr Kate Ames, Senior Lecturer, Professional Communication, Central Queensland University

Step Up is an aptly named book as its content includes key messages and strategies for opening the door to career success. Any person engaged in the management challenge should keep this book by their side and refer to it when their job becomes taxing or conflict emerges. The way we approach interacting with others is critical to workplace success.

With more than 200 references to risk management issues, the book will be especially relevant to the 12,000 or so Australian banking and financial services professionals who manage risk and compliance.

Richard Gilbert, Executive Director, Risk Management Association of Australia Inc

*To my husband, Craig Salisbury, for being there.
For listening to my ideas. For encouraging me.
For supporting me every step of the way.
For giving me the space and time to write this book.*

About the author

Michelle Gibbings is known for making the complex, simple. She helps people to think more deliberately, act with greater purpose and achieve more progress by understanding the art and science of change.

Michelle loves making change happen. She reframes how people experience change by strengthening their aspiration and ability to navigate through the complexity and influence outcomes. To her, change isn't a process. It's about critical moments, and having the skills to know what to do in each of those moments. In those critical moments there are turning points. You can do nothing, go straight ahead, take a detour, go left or right or just keep spinning around and get nowhere. Michelle helps people find their way through those turning points, so they can get the most out of changing environments.

With more than 20 years' experience in leading and guiding people through change in the public, private and not-for-profit sectors she knows how change works in different personal and organisational contexts. Her expertise is underpinned by success in designing and leading large-scale organisational change, having worked in a number of companies and financial institutions and in senior leadership positions at NAB and AMP. Her depth of experience extends across strategy, compliance, governance, and risk and program management.

Understanding the challenges and opportunities of orchestrating change in disruptive and shifting environments she offers practical ideas, blended with the latest thinking to optimise outcomes.

Michelle is also the Founder of Change Meridian, a consulting firm dedicated to helping people, teams and organisations get the most from change.

Michelle has undergraduate degrees in Communications and Commerce, and a Masters in International Trade. She is an Internationally Certified Compliance Professional by the International Federation of Compliance Associations, and is a graduate and member of the Australian Institute of Company Directors. She is also a Fellow of FINSIA, an Associate Fellow of the Australian Institute of Management, and a member of the Risk Management Association, the Governance, Risk and Compliance Institute and the Change Management Institute. She sits on the Board of the Arts Law Centre of Australia.

Contents

Acknowledgments	xiv
How to use this book	xv

1. Introduction   1
   Influence as competitive advantage   4
   The ladder of influence   6
   Applying the approach   9

PART 1: THE INDIVIDUAL

2. Own your mindset   19
   Interrogate your mindset   27
      Step One: Know your options   27
      Step Two: Assess your position   29
   Evolve your mindset   33
      Step One: Choose your paradigm   35
      Step Two: Explore the possibilities   39
      Step Three: Take action with practice   42

3. Strengthen your integrity   53
   Unplug your bias   59
      Step One: Elevate your awareness   62
      Step Two: Analyse your triggers and actions   67
      Step Three: Construct your aptitude   71

4. Be always agile	**79**
Master the game of progress	82
Step One: Be decisive	*83*
Step Two: Be disciplined	*89*
Step Three: Be determined	*92*
Stay ahead of the game	95
Step One: Embrace learning to change	*96*
Step Two: Learn with passion and reason	*99*
Step Three: Dominate your cravings	*103*

PART 2 – THE ORGANISATION

5. Activate the system	**109**
Know the system	112
Step One: Know the context for change	*112*
Step Two: Examine the culture	*117*
Step Three: Anchor your power base	*121*
Work the system	124
Step One: Keep it real	*125*
Step Two: Lead with purpose	*131*
Step Three: Leverage all angles	*134*

6. Appeal to human insight	**137**
The nature of motivation	140
Step One: Motivate with knowledge	*140*
Step Two: Motivate with progress	*146*
Step Three: Motivate during change	*149*
Create a new narrative	151
Step One: Lead consciously	*152*
Step Two: Lead individually	*157*
Step Three: Lead collectively	*162*

Nurture relationships	166
Step One: Build the foundation	*168*
Step Two: Construct your network	*171*
Step Three: Nourish your network	*177*
7. Craft impact	**181**
Communicate with influence	183
Step One: Cultivate the content	*185*
Step Two: Drive the delivery	*189*
Step Three: Perfect your timing	*192*
Negotiate wisely	194
Step One: Know the relationship landscape	*197*
Step Two: Be ready – craft the approach	*200*
Step Three: Have resolve and step up	*204*
8. What's next?	**209**
How to reach Michelle Gibbings	*211*
References	*212*
Index	*217*

Acknowledgments

It's said that it takes a village to raise a child, and I'd say that it takes a tribe to write a book. This book's creation is influenced by many people who have touched my life. To my parents, Michael and Rosemary, who encouraged a love of reading and learning from an early age. They've always had faith in my ability and encouraged me to do my best.

To the people who took the time to review the book and provide feedback: my sisters, Jenny Parer and Julie Robertson and my husband, Craig Salisbury. To the many people who provided feedback on the book's cover, including: Rosemary and Michael Gibbings, James Robertson, Rafferty Parer, Warwick Parer, Robyn Weatherley, Lynley Corcoran and Kate Badgery-Parker.

To Ann Crabb for her advice on the fine details of the publishing world. It was invaluable. To my good friend, Robyn Weatherley, who introduced me to her publisher, Lesley Williams, who in turn became my publisher. To Gabrielle Dolan and Craig Stephens, who introduced me to the Thought Leaders' community. The structure and process that Matt Church and Peter Cook have created to enable people to craft and share their intellectual property has helped make this book much better than it would have been otherwise. To my coach, Rod Buchecker who has been a fantastic support throughout the book's incubation. To Christina Guidotti for the reminder of the importance of sharing and to "write the book". And lastly, to Lesley Williams, thanks for taking on this project and being a voice of enthusiasm. Thanks to all of you for your advice and encouragement.

How to use this book

Change happens! Make it work for you.

That's a mantra that I live my life by. I believe there are skills, practices and techniques that individuals, teams and organisations can apply to make change work.

Everyone says that change is hard. Change isn't hard. We make it hard. We construct a mindset, and impose systems and processes that make change hard.

When I tell people that I'm a change expert they usually think about programmatic change. For example, when a new technology system is installed or a company restructures.

To me, change is much broader than that. In a nutshell, change is about getting stuff done. Sometimes the stuff to get done is big, and sometimes it's small. Sometimes the goal to reach is personal, and sometimes it's professionally based or organisationally driven.

To be influential in an organisation you need to be able to get stuff done, and you need to be able to get it done well. All of this needs to occur in an environment where the goalposts keep shifting and everything can feel as if it is in a constant state of flux.

It can feel exhausting. You may be wondering – when will it all end? When will it slow down? When do I get the time to just catch my breath? Sorry to disappoint you. There's no chance that the rate of change will get slower.

The only thing that can change is your capacity to cope with change and, if you're a leader, the capacity of your team to cope with change.

Organisations are going through rapid change and the most successful leaders are able to make the most of these dynamic environments. They understand themselves, understand others and understand how to best manage and motivate changes in behaviour. It is through these core skills that they are able to prosper through change, and gather the influence they need to be successful.

These skills are relevant for everyone – regardless of their role or hierarchical position or industry sector.

There are lots of books on change, so what makes this book different?

Step Up is written for people who are more technically focused but are at that stage in their career where they know they need more skills – of a different nature – if they want to advance. The time at which this need arises will differ for people. Some people may have been working in an organisation for years, while for others it will be less. Technically focused professionals come from all walks of life and many different technical domains. They can be accountants, HR practitioners, marketing specialists, change managers, financial planners, risk management experts, technologists, project managers, financial controllers, engineers, scientists or even doctors. They are people who connect with their technical craft first, even though they may now be in a leadership role (or are aspiring to be).

If you want to make the most out of changing circumstances and gain greater traction at work, you need to be able to influence. You need to be able to step up and into your power. And by that I mean an 'inner sense of power' that comes with the confidence of knowing that you have the requisite skills to be successful and to hold your own with your peers and those more senior than you.

If you are in a leadership position, or aspire to hold a leadership position, how do you respond when someone asks you what you do? Do you define yourself by your technical profession, or your leadership position? Are you more comfortable with the technical elements of your role than the leadership elements?

If you put the technical side first, then this book is for you.

Throughout my career, I've worked with technicians. They're masters of their functional domain. However, some of them really struggled to be heard and to be a key influencer in the organisation. They struggled to get traction. They struggled to make change happen.

And there were others, who had enormous impact. They were able to work with and through people. They were able to leverage a situation to make it work for them, and they had a positive impact on those around them. The difference was their ability to communicate with influence, negotiate outcomes and build awesome stakeholder relationships. They operated, often subconsciously, as change agents in the organisation. And most importantly, they were able to build coalitions of support, create engaged teams and deliver on commitments. In short, they had influence and power, and they knew how to use it wisely.

Of course, there were also people who were very influential, but they used this influence for personal gain, not for the greater good. They influenced for their own end and gain. You know the person – all talk no action. For them power is an aphrodisiac. They spend their time in the organisation managing up and never getting anything done that helped those around them, or the broader organisation. Instead, it was all about helping themselves. They lacked integrity and everything they did was with an eye to their next promotion.

This is the person who spends their life managing up and ensuring that they look good, often at the expense of others. They're no-one to aspire to – and they're no asset to the organisation.

So when I talk about influence and stepping into your power I'm not advocating that you strive to be that type of person.

Imagine how good it would be if people who had the technical skills, but who felt they lacked the skills to influence, acquired more influence. Think of it like balancing the scales. And I want to tip the scales in favour of those people in organisations who for many years have felt as if they have gone unheard, and that their voices have been drowned out by the charismatic leader or the classic extrovert who has all the answers and is never shy of putting them forward.

To tip the scales in your favour and be more influential you need to move beyond the technical to a behaviourally focused approach. A behavioural focus has an enormously positive impact on the ability of professionals to get things done and to get traction in organisations. This is because understanding the nature of yourself and others better positions you to navigate the complexities of changing organisations.

Organisations today are going through an unprecedented scale and volume of change. Successful organisations know they need to keep changing to survive. If you are to be a successful leader in an organisation, not only do you need to know how you can change, but you need to be able to shepherd others through change. This requires you to be able to identify and manage your way through the critical moments of change.

To build a platform for influence a purely technical focus just doesn't cut it.

Step Up is practically focused and theoretically based. Every idea that is presented has at its core some form of scientific research or evidence that backs up the position. It includes practical steps you can take to build your platform for influence.

This book has been written so it can be easily digested. This means that while most people will read the book from start to finish, it can be started from any chapter; as each chapter is stand-alone. Experience has shown that people will respond to the ideas in this book differently. There will be some areas that resonate strongly and others less so. Take the time to find what works for you. The ideas in this book work, but they are only effective if you put them into practice.

You will first be introduced to the framework that underpins this book. The framework provides the core building blocks that are necessary for you to create a platform for influence.

The book examines the subject of change from two perspectives – the individual and the organisation. The first section of the book looks at this from an individual perspective. It explains the impact of your mindset on your thinking and behaviour, and then helps you uncover your operating style and integrity base. Understanding yourself, before you try and understand other people, is critical. This section also considers the steps you can take to make progress and stay ahead of the game in an organisation. This is another critical step because progress leads to success, and consequently, helps to build influence.

The second section of the book looks at the individual's role in an organisational setting. It discusses why it's important to have clarity on the organisational system and culture in which you are working, and what you need to do to make the most of it. The book then shares key behavioural insights into how you can nurture great relationships and motivate behavioural change. Leaders can't deliver change alone. They secure organisational change by motivating and supporting those around them to achieve success. Two core skills that are required for this are being able to communicate with influence and negotiate wisely. These skills are outlined in detail.

I've really enjoyed writing this book, and I wish you every happiness as you read it and use the techniques in your personal and professional life. As you embark on this quest reflect on the quote from Mark Twain: *"Success is a journey, not a destination. It requires constant effort, vigilance and re-evaluation*". This is your opportunity to step into your power, and step up to have the career you want and deserve.

Above all else, enjoy the experience. Just as change happens, so life happens. Make that work for you too!

With my best wishes for a happy, healthy, productive and fulfilling life.

MICHELLE

P.S. I'd love to hear your stories and feedback on this book, so I can include them in the next edition. Please leave your feedback at michelle@michellegibbings.com.

1. Introduction

> "If we did all the things we are capable of doing, we would literally astound ourselves."
>
> —*Thomas Edison, Inventor*

Mid-way through my career I moved into risk and compliance. This was a deliberate move that surprised many people. Before I moved into risk and compliance I had been working in an advisory role for the CEO. Risk and compliance certainly wasn't seen as the sexy part of the organisation, nor an area that had much influence. I remember people asking me why I had gone to work with the 'cardigan brigade', and questioned why I wanted to work in an area that was the 'handbrake on happiness'. The cardigan was a reference to a biased perception that risk and compliance professionals weren't 'cool', but highly analytical and so perhaps a little boring. While the handbrake comment reflected a view that the risk and compliance team was just there to say "no", and therefore interaction with them was a hindrance not a help.

The comments may have been light-hearted but the perception that lay behind those sentiments was all too real. To many people, risk and compliance was seen as an afterthought. It was not regarded as a central part of the business. It wasn't seen as a place to go to grow your career. This is funny when you think that I was working in a financial institution, which is all about risk – how much you take, where you take it, and how you manage it.

The challenge was that risk and compliance often attracted people who were highly technically competent, but they weren't good at negotiating outcomes or influencing stakeholders. Some of them knew this was a gap, while others were blissfully unaware.

And so this is how it would play out…

There was often tension between the revenue-generating areas of the business (that just wanted to get on, hit targets and make money) and risk and compliance folk (who were trying to rein in those activities). But, it's hard to rein something in when you don't know how to influence. Of course, there were legal and compliance requirements that needed to be met, but relying on that argument to secure influence only got you so far.

Motivating someone to do something through fear (or a reward) is not a long-term strategy. Playing the role with a big stick in your hand isn't the way to build a long-term, healthy relationship either. At the same time, you worry that if you push issues too hard with the business you'll 'burn' relationships.

When I worked as the Head of Compliance I would often have business leaders complaining to me that the compliance person they were dealing with didn't understand the business and wasn't helping them. The person did understand the business, but they struggled to communicate effectively and didn't know how to position arguments in a way that they could be heard. This made getting things done and working with the business harder than it needed to be.

While I've used a risk and compliance example here, this challenge translates across many technical roles. People in technically driven and functionally focused roles often struggle to get heard in organisations.

It may be the financial controller who knows that the sales projections don't look right but has difficulty convincing the executive team to take notice and action. It may be the procurement head who can see that the organisation would be more effective with its suppliers if it changed how it interacted with them. It may be the data specialist who can see issues with the organisation's strategy but doesn't know how to position their concerns. It may be a junior marketing manager who wants to suggest changes to the organisation's advertising strategy but doesn't feel confident in pitching the message. The examples are numerous.

In all cases, these people are struggling to get heard – ultimately hampering their ability to make progress and to be seen as a successful leader.

When you find yourself in this situation, you can feel exiled from the people who hold the power in the organisation. You feel left behind. Out of the loop. Unimportant. You feel as if you have no power. It's not a good place to be.

If you think about it, you're not in the driver's seat. You're the passenger, and sometimes perhaps you're not even the passenger in the front seat who is helping to navigate. You're in the back seat with no ability to influence the direction and speed of the journey, or the route taken.

☑ CHECKPOINT ACTIVITY

Do you sometimes struggle to:

- ☐ Get your point across in meetings?
- ☐ Build long-term, constructive relationships with senior executives and colleagues?
- ☐ Develop a coalition of support for a concept from idea through to implementation?

- ☐ Understand what motivates you and others to action?
- ☐ Construct engaged and effective teams that can successfully navigate complexity and change?
- ☐ Negotiate clear and balanced outcomes?
- ☐ Know when to hold your ground, give up ground or walk away from a debate?
- ☐ Get things done in your organisation?

If you answered yes to any of these questions don't be discouraged. There is another way. A better way.

From my experience, getting traction and getting your stakeholders and colleagues to listen is about gaining influence, understanding how power works in an organisation and using both of these elements wisely.

INFLUENCE AS COMPETITIVE ADVANTAGE

Most people when they hear the term 'competitive advantage' think about Michael Porter's definition as it relates to organisations. That is, for an organisation to succeed it needs to know what it's good at vis-à-vis other players in the market. It's this point of difference and how it is leveraged that makes an organisation stand out and succeed.

Every individual has a unique set of skills. You can hone your skills in a way to create your distinct competitive advantage. To secure this competitive advantage, your professional toolkit needs to go beyond the traditional – to include an ability to motivate and encourage behavioural change and secure outcomes. In short, you need to be able to influence.

If you look at successful leaders – in business, society and politics – they all know how to influence. They know how to get things done through other people and are aware of the environment in which they are operating. They know how to use their personal power to secure outcomes.

On a daily basis, business executives are bombarded with information and requests. When I was a senior executive I'd regularly receive over 300 emails a day. I'd also often spend eight hours in back-to-back meetings. My husband who's an IT specialist could never understand it. He used to say to me: "How can you possibly spend all day in meetings? What are you actually achieving?" The sad thing was often we weren't achieving as much as we could have been.

I was often overwhelmed with information. It's what noted economist and Nobel Prize winner, Herbert Simon sees as a "wealth of information" creating "a poverty of attention".[1] There's so much information that it's hard to get through it and know what to focus on.

The only way I could survive the information onslaught was to be ruthless about what I spent my time on. Processes and activities which couldn't be explicitly connected with delivering value and business outcomes were pushed down the priority list.

There was immense value in working with people who were able to help me sift through the rubble to find the gems I needed to focus on. People who just gave me more information and no insights were less helpful. Similarly, in dealing with my business stakeholders I knew that for the relationship to be of value to them, I needed to offer insights so I could play a critical role in helping them grow their business and achieve their outcomes. The relationship needed to be more about them and their needs, and less about my needs. By shifting the focus to them, I would ultimately get what I needed.

The people who influenced me were often the people who helped make my working life easier. This didn't mean they were sycophants who never expressed a different view. Their opinions were valuable. They were influential because they were constantly adding value – and often more than they were expected to. They understood what it took to craft personal influence.

THE LADDER OF INFLUENCE

Everyone in an organisation has a label. This label is often your role title. Unfortunately, role titles can box people in. If you're a communications manager, you're the comms person. If you're the financial controller, you're the finance person. If you're the systems engineer, you're the technical person. This is despite the fact that your experience may extend well beyond those titles.

While you have a designated role in your organisation – that comes with your title – it's up to you to choose what level of influence you want to hold.

At this point you may be thinking – "Yeah right, I can't determine my own level of influence". I'd argue that you can. But, it's about how much you are willing to do things differently.

Ask yourself: how much effort am I willing to put into learning and changing my mindset and adopting a behavioural approach to leadership? How much am I willing to do things differently so I step into my personal power?

I'd argue you have choice, but I'd also argue that today's disruptive environmental context dictates that you need to take a different approach.

Assessing your position

Looking at Figure 1, consider where you are placed with regard to your position of influence and where you want to be. Do you want to be at the bottom of the scale and be a 'plodder' who is pedestrian and not having much impact? Or at the top and be a catalyst for progress in your organisation? Catalysts know how to influence and know how to get things done – adding ten times the amount of value for the organisation and their own career.

Figure 1: Positions of influence in today's environmental context

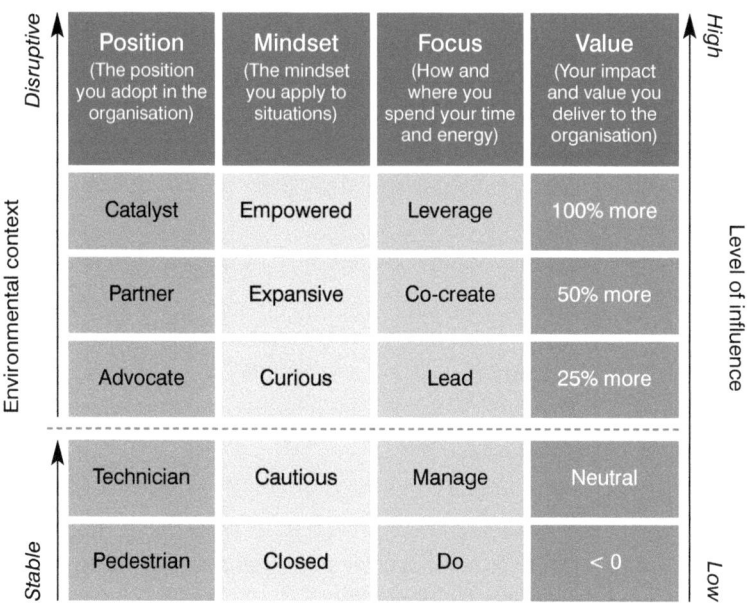

Let's start with assessing where you are now. For this to work you need to be honest with yourself. Everyone can do better, and this exercise is just about finding out how you are currently positioned.

Additionally, be willing to ask people their opinion, and how they would answer the question on your behalf so that you get some different perspectives to work with.

☑ CHECKPOINT ACTIVITY

Ask yourself:

- ☐ Am I regularly sought out for my opinion?
- ☐ Do I provide an independent voice and confidently put forward views that are different to those of people senior to me?

- [ ] Am I able to successfully resolve difficult conversations and negotiate outcomes with people more senior than me?
- [ ] Do I look beyond my role (and my team) to see the connections/dependencies with other areas of the organisation so I can take a whole-of-organisation perspective when making decisions?
- [ ] Do I know how to navigate the organisation's complexity to get things done?
- [ ] Do I take a systems-based perspective to issues I am facing in the organisation?
- [ ] Do I have an effective balance of business astuteness, technical skill and behavioural awareness?
- [ ] Do I take a long-term view of relationships so I can build a sustainable network?
- [ ] Do I seek to operate beyond the domain of my current role to ensure effective outcomes and deliver beyond expectations?
- [ ] Am I comfortable to leverage my personal power and do I know how to do this for best effect?
- [ ] Do I understand how power works in the organisation and how to leverage it?
- [ ] Do I seek to continually stay ahead of the game in terms of knowledge and understanding how disruptive forces are working in my industry?
- [ ] Am I constantly pushing myself to try new things and to improve the way things are done around the organisation?
- [ ] Do I openly embrace change and the challenges and opportunities that come with it?
- [ ] Am I skilled at successfully supporting my team (if I have one) and those around me through ambiguity and uncertainty?

For every question that you answered yes, give yourself one point. Then tally up the points and see where you currently stand.

Remember, this also needs to be done contextually. There is power, rank and hierarchy in an organisation that will impact the degree of influence you have. If you're in a junior position or at entry level management, you can't realistically expect to have the same level of influence as an executive. But, you can have influence beyond that of other entry level managers. Consequently, regardless of your position in the organisation you can either wield more or less power and influence based on your mindset and the actions you take.

> **STEP UP TIP**
> This will be a useless exercise if you fall into the Dunning Kruger effect. This is a cognitive bias where unskilled people over-estimate their ability and have delusions of their superior capability.

Take a look at Figure 2 overleaf to see how you rate.

As you move up the ladder of influence you become more adept at knowing the right time to listen and challenge, and the right time to act. You'll be skilled at using all aspects of this influence model to secure the best outcome for the organisation and its stakeholders. And in turn, you'll increase the amount of value you provide, and therefore the value you secure for your career.

APPLYING THE APPROACH

If you want to move up the ladder of influence there are a number of things you can do.

This book will unpack each of these elements and provide you with new ideas and learnings to help you become more influential. A useful starting point is to outline the framework that will underpin this learning. Frameworks are helpful as they provide a way of structuring information and ideas, and so become a useful reference point as the book progresses. This framework recognises that there are layers of understanding and different contexts in

Figure 2: Your position on the ladder of influence

Score (out of 15)	Position on the ladder of influence
0 to 3	**Pedestrian** – the professional is focused on reactive tasks and has limited ability to provide proactive advice or guidance to stakeholders. The role is purely process and task based. Influence levels are low.
4 to 6	**Technician** – the professional's role is operational and functionally focused. They may be called in reactively when things go wrong or when information they hold is needed. There is some ability to provide proactive advice and guidance to stakeholders. They are not seen as an enabler of change in the organisation and have limited influence.
6 to 10	**Advocate** – the professional leads directionally but finds it hard to build a coalition of support particularly on matters beyond their domain of expertise. They can advocate or support change, but they are not a catalyst for change. They add value to the business and its operations in a systematic fashion. They have some ability to influence outcomes.
11 to 13	**Partner** – the professional is comfortable challenging stakeholders more senior than them. They proactively seek to advise the organisation and have good relationships with key stakeholders. They are able to influence beyond the domain of their role and are seen as a strategic enabler of change in the organisation. They seek to co-create long-term sustainable outcomes.
14 to 15	**Catalyst** – the professional operates with long-term competitive advantage in disruptive and ambiguous environments. They help to generate sustainable organisational outcomes, operate as a key part of the organisation's decision making hierarchy and know how to leverage the system for best effect. They can comfortably provide the necessary voice of independent thinking. They challenge and their voice is heard. They are a 'go to' person for issues and advice beyond the domain of their role. They are highly influential.

which an individual operates. Each layer needs to be unpacked and understood.

The starting point for this discovery is the inner circle of the framework, which is your mindset. This concept is core to the learning. This is because mindsets impact the way you think and ultimately act. The assumptions that underpin your mindset create blind spots and biases that can have serious consequences for relationships, decision-making and ultimately outcomes.

Of course, it's not only about your mindset. It's also about gaining an understanding of other people's mindsets. In an organisational context, this mix of mindsets is often brought to life through the organisation's culture. This might sound odd. How can mindsets make a culture? Easily.

The executive team's behaviour, what they say and don't say, and what they do and don't do are ingredients that make up the organisation's culture. And, much of their behaviour is driven by their individual mindsets. However, collectively, individuals in a team influence each other and over time they can create a collective mindset, so that each member of the team starts to think and act in the same way. This social conditioning can either be a force for good or not so good.

This is critical to understand as no individual, team or organisation operates in a vacuum. They operate as part of a system, and the culture dominates how that system operates. The system is like a hidden force that impedes or prevents change from happening. Consequently, the system can have a huge impact on how you influence and its effectiveness.

In addition to your mindset, which is at the core, and the cultural system, which is all pervasive, there are two primary dimensions at play: environment and focus.

The ENVIRONMENT is either centred on the individual or the

organisation. This is an important distinction as you need to first understand yourself to then be able to understand others.

To be successful you need to stay true to yourself and operate with integrity. This involves understanding your value drivers and triggers, and being able to recognise when those values are at risk.

You also need to be able to successfully operate in an organisational context. You will be more valued by the organisation if you have insight into people and know how to get things done through people. Importantly, this is about gaining perspective on people and how they are best motivated, and then knowing what to do with that knowledge.

These elements work together because if you are operating with integrity and have insight, your approach naturally goes beyond the 'winner takes all' strategy. It is much more about shared value for all stakeholders. This is essential for successfully negotiating, making progress and building your influence.

The second dimension is FOCUS. At one end of the spectrum the focus is on thinking, while at the other end it is on doing. Of course, often these two elements occur at the same time. It's useful to think about them separately because if you are to go to a deeper level of understanding you will want to think before you act. In this way you will give attention to both the thought processes you use, as well as the action you take. To do this you not only need to understand yourself and what drives you, but you need to stay true to your values, and to think and act with integrity.

Additionally you want to be agile. This is about acting decisively, being coherent and well planned. It's about being responsive to changing circumstances, and flexible to accommodate the opinions and needs of others. Being agile will help you stay on track and stay ahead of the game – always. This is imperative. In today's disruptive environment the track keeps moving and the curve keeps shifting. By staying ahead of the curve and delivering fresh and insightful perspective at the right time and in the right way you'll have greater impact on stakeholders, and over time, greater impact on decision-making processes and outcomes.

Having impact that is healthy, helpful and heroic is the goal. This is not a self-serving impact that is all about you. It is much more altruistic. It is about impact that delivers the best value to all stakeholders and the organisation. Research shows that consumers are much more engaged with organisations that have good reputations, and that employees want to work for organisations that take their community and social responsibilities seriously.

This book's framework is presented graphically below (see Figure 3).

This book is based on the premise that you desire to learn more and to change in some way. Are you ready?

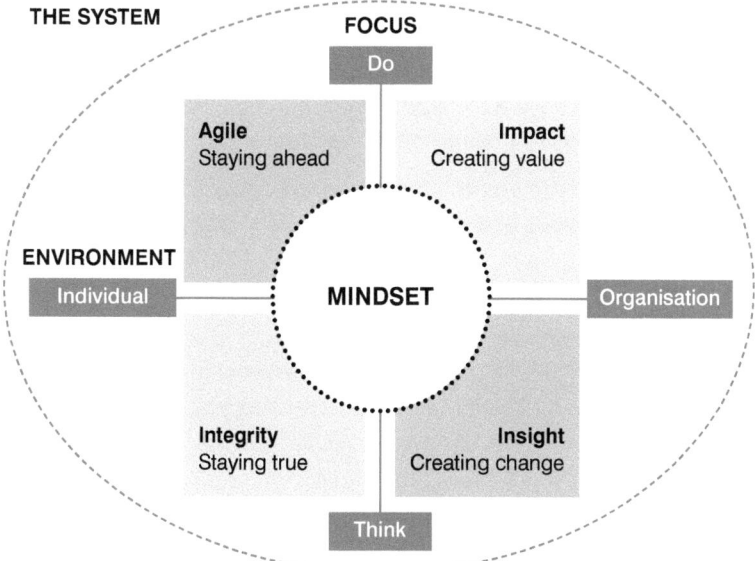

Figure 3: The framework for building your influence at work

☑ CHECKPOINT ACTIVITY

Ask yourself:

- [ ] How physically, mentally and emotionally resilient are you? This is about uncovering your bandwidth for change – its depth and breadth. The more flexible and adaptable you are, the more likely you are to welcome this personal change and see it as invigorating.

- [ ] Are you willing to invest the necessary time and energy to acquire these new skills and capabilities? Learning new skills and acquiring additional capabilities takes commitment and effort.

- [ ] How tolerant are you of ambiguity and disorder? Personal change doesn't occur in isolation from what is happening around you. We live in a world of instability, uncertainty and disruption. The more you are able to thrive in it, the less destabilising you'll find it.

- [ ] How do you react when things go wrong? Personal change always involves learning and experimentation, and things invariably don't always go according to plan. How you react to mistakes and your ability to learn from them are hallmarks of whether you have a fixed or growth mindset. Having a growth mindset is key to making personal change.

- [ ] How attuned are you to others and their needs? This is about broadening your field of view so you don't only focus on what this change means for you, but you look around and consider the impact on others.

- [ ] Are you emotionally invested in wanting to change? Do you care enough, too much or not all? Your level of emotional investment will determine how much effort you put into making the change work for you and those around you.

How did you go?

Much of how you answered would have been driven by your mindset. So why does your mindset matter? Let me explain…

I've been fortunate in my career to have moved across functions. Starting in corporate affairs, I moved into advisory work, compliance, risk, strategy and organisational change. I was often asked about how I did it. What drove the enquiry was a curiosity as to how I was able to move across functional disciplines when I didn't have the underlying technical expertise.

My answer was that I wasn't being hired for my technical skills. I was being hired because of my ability to get stuff done, and my ability to influence stakeholders and manage and motivate behavioural change. I became comfortable with power and how to use it. I wasn't born with these skills. I learnt them and the mindset I applied was critical in being able to do this.

Your mindset is at the centre of everything you do. If it's not aligned to what you need, you'll end up in the wrong location.

In the next part of *Step Up* you'll start to uncover the key elements of your mindset and what could be holding you back.

Part 1
The Individual

2. Own your mindset

> "Our experience is not what happens to us, but what we make of what happens to us."
> —*Aldous Huxley, Author*

Everyone's mindset is unique, and it is crafted over time. Your mindset is shaped by your experience. It is an important part of who you are and it impacts what you think and how you behave. This is because you are interpreting the world and what is happening through the lens of past experience – *your* past experience.

It is these past experiences that ultimately shape your beliefs and perceptions of what, for example, is right or wrong. From that position you make assumptions about how things should be – not necessarily how they are. It is this gap between your perception and reality that gives rise to blind spots. Because you expect something to be a certain way you can miss what is really going on. Your unique world view drives your internal state, and ultimately your thoughts, emotions and behaviour.

Think of it like the ageing process for red wine. If the environmental conditions and inputs into the process are poor, the wine will age badly. But, if the conditions are good and the inputs are well selected, the wine will age well.

Your mind is the same. The concept of 'garbage in–garbage out' fits perfectly. If your mind is closed to new experiences and ideas it will be unable to cope in new situations and struggle to embrace what is going on around you. If however, your mind is open to challenge and different opinions it will be much more readily able to cope with changing circumstances.

It's important to be critically aware of the mindset you are taking into situations, particularly when you are making decisions and trying to build new relationships. You need to consider the impact that your mindset may have on the outcome, and whether it will detract or enhance the situation.

> **STEP UP TIP**
>
> A quick way to check your mindset is to ask yourself the following question: *Do you believe that you know everything you need to know already, or do you believe that there is still so much to learn?*
>
> How you answer will help you determine if you have a fixed or growth mindset.

These terms were coined by the world renowned Stanford academic, Carol Dweck.[2] She found that people who have a fixed mindset see intelligence as static – a fixed trait. As a result, they want to always look smart and appear as though they have all the answers. They believe that success is based on talent alone – not the effort they put into the task.

People with a fixed mindset are more likely to avoid challenges and give up more easily. They think they know everything and so are more likely to ignore feedback. They also see feedback as a criticism and feel threatened by the success of others.

In contrast, people with a growth mindset believe that intelligence can be developed through hard work and effort. Consequently, they are more eager to embrace learning, take on challenges and persist, despite setbacks. They love learning and are more willing to learn from others. Crucially, they're happy to take on feedback and have greater resilience.

The danger is that your mindset can limit you and in ways you may not be consciously aware of. It can put in place roadblocks and obstacles that make it much harder to achieve your objectives. Or worse, it may lead you down a path where your 'faulty thinking' (i.e. assumptions and blind spots) creates 'faulty choice' (i.e. decisions) and ultimately delivers a 'faulty outcome' (see Figure 4 below).

Figure 4: A faulty mindset in action

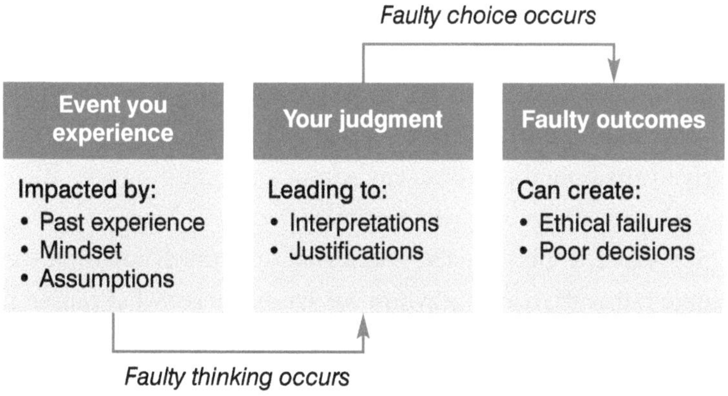

Faulty choice occurs

Event you experience	Your judgment	Faulty outcomes
Impacted by: • Past experience • Mindset • Assumptions	Leading to: • Interpretations • Justifications	Can create: • Ethical failures • Poor decisions

Faulty thinking occurs

How this works in practice is that your mindset is based on assumptions; assumptions as to what should happen or what is right or wrong. When new information is presented you can ignore that information or discard it, because it doesn't fit with your view of the world.

When you do that you are subconsciously creating a blind spot that prevents you from factoring this new information into the decision being made. Consequently, your judgment becomes impaired, which in turn leads to a faulty decision being made, with potentially faulty consequences.

These pitfalls can have significant consequences for the decisions you make. This is discussed in more detail in Chapter 3, in the section 'Unplug your bias' (see page 59). At this point, it's just relevant for you to know that your mindset is your construction. And so it is yours to change as well.

But, the problems don't end there.

The inner voice inside your head can be pretty noisy at times. It can easily lead you astray. Unfortunately, it's a poor evaluator of what is really going on.

Many of you will have heard of the concept 'fundamental attribution error'. It's where you attribute the error that another person makes to *them*. If *they* do something wrong it's because "they're stupid" or "what an idiot". It's not situational.

Whereas when the same thing happens to you, you're far more likely to attribute the error to environmental circumstances. It's like the old proverb: "A bad worker blames their tools".

It's easier to blame what is external to yourself for what went wrong, rather than look at your own actions to see what caused the problem. This is normal human behaviour. The problem of course is you don't judge yourself in the same way you judge others.

I've seen this happen plenty of times in an organisation (and I've been guilty of it too), particularly when I was moving into a new team environment. As the new team leader, I would invariably have people give me their opinions on people in the team. These opinions were not just their assessment on the person's capability but also their assessment on the person's personality, style and behaviour. I learnt over time to ignore those opinions – as they were invariably wrong. Many times, the people who I was told were "no good", ended up being the star performers in the team (and vice versa). A person's ability and skill were situational and not fixed because they were influenced by the environment they were working in and their relationship with their manager.

If something goes wrong you can end up with quite contradictory thoughts and behaviour. On one hand, you may want to shy away and try and deflect blame to something or someone else. But, at other times your inner voice can be an incredibly harsh critic. It can make it harder for you to cope with change and new circumstances because it dredges up uncertainties. It questions your actions. It raises doubt. It worries. It's overly negative.

Your brain is constantly filtering information and rapidly trying to make sense of the world and what is going on around you. It filters out information it thinks is extraneous and takes short-cuts to get to an answer. This helps you process information and situations quickly, but it also means you can be processing incorrectly.

For example, think of the following scenarios:

- Your team leader has decided to do something you disagree with. They're trying to explain their point of view, and it's diametrically opposed to your view. In your head you are saying: "I can't believe they're doing this. It is such a bad idea". At this point you've probably stopped listening. Your fixed view of the world is closing you off to other ideas. Seeing the world as 'black or white', 'right or wrong' and having no middle ground can lead you to being oblivious to what is really happening.

- You've planned a weekend away with your partner, and rather than having sunshine you're having torrential rain. In your head you're saying: "Oh this weather is dreadful, it will ruin my weekend". You can find yourself over-exaggerating the negative consequences because your mind can be more attuned to the negative.

- You've gone to a party with a group of friends and one of your friends doesn't talk to you. What goes on in your head? Do you think about what is going on for them, or are you thinking: "They just ignored me, they mustn't like me anymore". You can easily personalise situations and make it about you, when in fact the person's reaction or the situation may have nothing to do with you.

- You're working with a colleague who is disorganised and has forgotten to do something that impacts on your joint project. In your head you may be saying: "What a stuff up. They've got no ability to plan". Your brain is a meaning-seeking machine and is always trying to rapidly make sense of the world and so it can make quick conclusions based on limited information.

In each of those scenarios there are very plausible alternatives. The team leader's decision may be based on facts that you don't know about. The rain may mean you stay indoors and read a book that has a profound effect on you. Your friend may have a lot going on for them personally. And lastly, your colleague may plan in a way that is different to how you plan.

Just because you have a view doesn't mean that it's the right one.

The danger of course is when you let your inner voice take control and run the show.

Figure 5 shows how this can play out…

Figure 5: Your inner voice as saboteur

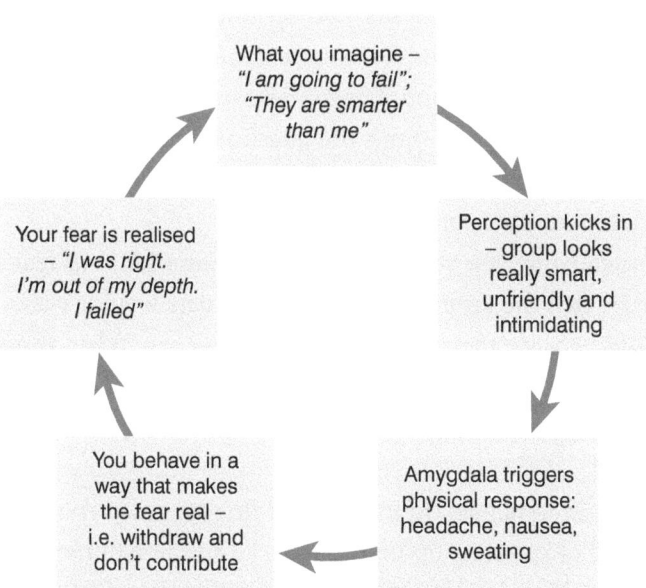

Let's take an example to explain the diagram above. You are heading into a meeting with a group of stakeholders who are more senior than you. That situation, in of itself, can be quite intimidating. Naturally, your inner voice is on guard and wary. It's nervous and not wanting you to stuff up. But, it's also telling you that you're not good enough and that these people are smarter than you. Your perception then kicks in and goes up a few gears as the meeting progresses. It starts to reinforce the voice in your head that the stakeholders are smart and you are out of your depth. This causes a chemical reaction in your brain and your 'fight or flight' senses go into action. This is often known as the 'amygdala hijack'. It manifests itself in a physical response. You may start sweating or feel nauseous. This isn't good for you on multiple levels.

The physical response then transitions into a behavioural

response. Your nerves start to overwhelm you, and you start to withdraw. You limit what you say. You act differently to the way you would normally act if you were more confident. The stakeholders notice your withdrawal and changed behaviour. They start responding to that and begin to limit the questions they ask you. As this happens your involvement becomes less and less, and your fear becomes more and more realised.

Consequently you walk out of the meeting with your fear fully realised – that the group of senior stakeholders wouldn't take you seriously because they are smarter than you are. What you have ignored is the fact that you set yourself up for this failure. It was a self-fulfilling prophecy. You thought you were going to stuff up and so you did.

This used to happen to me. When I first started corporate life I was scared of speaking up in meetings. I'd sit there thinking about what to say. The meeting would go on and I'd still be silent. It made the situation worse. The longer I sat there silent, the more anxious I became about speaking up. It was horrible. It took me years to get over this. The 'getting over it' was forced on me as I moved into a role where I needed to present to senior executives. Before the presentation I felt as if I wanted to throw up. Of course I didn't and surprisingly the presentation would go well. Over time, I became more confident. As my confidence increased so too did my courage to speak up.

If you don't find a way to rein in your inner voice it can be a vicious cycle. This isn't easy, as it involves personal change. Personal change has two main stages. First you need to alter your mindset, and then alter your action.

The pre-conditions for this are to understand where you are placed currently. That is, are you ready to change your mindset? What's your level of desire and capacity to change?

From there you are ready to understand and learn the actions you can put into place to have a mindset that sets the stage for you to successfully embrace the innate power that resides within you. These actions are about seeking out and changing your paradigms, exploring possibilities and adopting new practices.

INTERROGATE YOUR MINDSET

> "However long the night, the dawn will break."
> —*African Proverb*

William Shakespeare's play "As You Like It" used the metaphor of the role you play in life as a stage. The melancholy nobleman, Jaques, says to Duke Senior:

All the world's a stage,
And all the men and women merely players.
They have their exits and their entrances,
And one man in his time plays many parts…

So if all the world's a stage and you are merely a player, do you get to choose the role you take on? Can the role you take on change over time?

The obvious answer to those questions is "Yes". You can choose the role you want to play. Do you want to be the victim? The hero or heroine? The side player or a main character? Who is writing the script for your life? Are you in charge of it, or have you outsourced it to someone else? It's your choice.

STEP ONE: Know your options

To understand your options, let's examine your awareness and willingness to change through two lenses:

1. **Consciousness:** Your level of awareness about your need to change
2. **Comfort zone:** Your risk appetite and tolerance for change.

This will determine your stage of development with respect to change and whether you are stagnating, reviving or thriving.

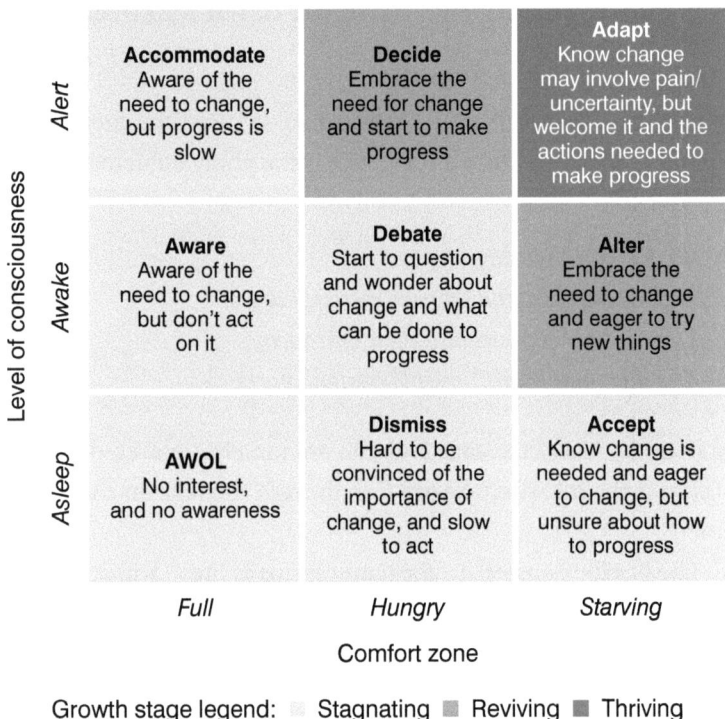

Figure 6: Examine your awareness and willingness to change

Level of consciousness

With all forms of change, it's important to be conscious of what is happening and to be involved as much as possible. There's a choice and decision to be made. With choice comes action and consequences.

But, before that there needs to be awareness. Awareness is about raising your consciousness. The more conscious you are of what is going on around you, the more you are able to be open to it, and over time, accepting of it. There are levels of consciousness. At the lowest end, you're asleep and you are not aware of what is happening and how your mind is processing these happenings. The next level is awake where you are aware and able to distinguish between what is happening and your interpretation of it. The last level is alert where your consciousness is at a heightened level of awareness and your mind is fully present and open to change.

Comfort zone

Some people embrace change. It's as if they're starving for it. They have a high risk appetite for new things, and find change relatively easy. In fact, doing new things – particularly risky things – provides an adrenalin rush and keeps them stimulated. In this context, risky doesn't necessarily mean dangerous, but it means they are willing to push the boundaries and try new things. At the other extreme, there are people who avoid all forms of change. They're not hungry at all. They've had their fill of change and they feel they are 'done' with it. They find it hard and so they avoid change, learning and any form of personal growth, even to their own detriment.

Growth stage

Depending on where you are placed on this table you will be stagnating, reviving or thriving. These are characterised as stages of growth because as your mind becomes more open you are able to alter your behaviour more easily. You can move from reflecting on what is happening, to processing what you need to do and trying new ways of thinking and acting, to making fundamental shifts that go beyond minor alterations to adaptation and transformation.

STEP TWO: Assess your position

It's now time to consider how you would rate yourself.

☑ CHECKPOINT ACTIVITY

Ask yourself:

Level of consciousness

- ☐ Do I meditate frequently (at least once a week, ideally daily)?
- ☐ Do I keep a journal to capture thoughts and reflections?
- ☐ Do I reflect on my thought processes, assumptions and decisions?
- ☐ Do I seek feedback from others on how they see my actions?
- ☐ Am I open to criticism and feedback, such that I act on it?
- ☐ Am I naturally curious about my mindset – the foundations, assumptions and blind spots that reside within it?
- ☐ Do I feel that I have so much more to learn?
- ☐ Do I see personal growth as necessary to my personal success?
- ☐ Am I looking for new ways to improve myself – every day?
- ☐ Do I have clear personal goals for development?
- ☐ Am I excited about the opportunity for personal growth?
- ☐ Do I have a plan that I can implement to support my personal growth goals?

Add up the number of 'yes' answers to determine your position on the vertical axis: 10 to 12 points places you on the top line; 1 to 6 on the bottom line; and 7 to 9 on the middle line (refer to Figure 6).

Comfort zone

- ☐ Does the thought of trying something new excite me?
- ☐ Do I embrace the motto: "feel the fear but do it anyway"?
- ☐ Am I willing to try things that I haven't done before even if I am not 100% sure that I will be successful?

- ☐ Do I regularly do things that I haven't done before?
- ☐ Am I frequently seeking out new things to learn and different things to do?
- ☐ Do I take the time to understand the need for change before seeking change?
- ☐ Do I understand that with learning comes risk, and that risk is essential for personal growth?
- ☐ Do I find the thought of organisational change exciting, and personal growth energising?
- ☐ Do I find the actions involved in personal change a good use of my time?
- ☐ Do I recognise that feeling discomfort is a sign of personal growth?
- ☐ Do I embrace change as a key enabler of my growth and future career success?
- ☐ Am I willing to always look for new ways to do things and to be the first to try something?

Add up the number of 'yes' answers to determine your position on the horizontal axis: 10 to 12 points places you on the top line; 1 to 6 on the bottom line; and 7 to 9 on the middle line.

Once you have these two numbers you can find the point of intersection between the horizontal and vertical axes to determine your position.

For an example, please refer to Figure 7 below. In this example, the person has rated themselves as between 7 and 9 for consciousness, and 10 and 12 for comfort zone. This means they are at the 'Alter' phase where they are embracing the need to change, and eager to try new things. They are reviving, but not yet thriving through change.

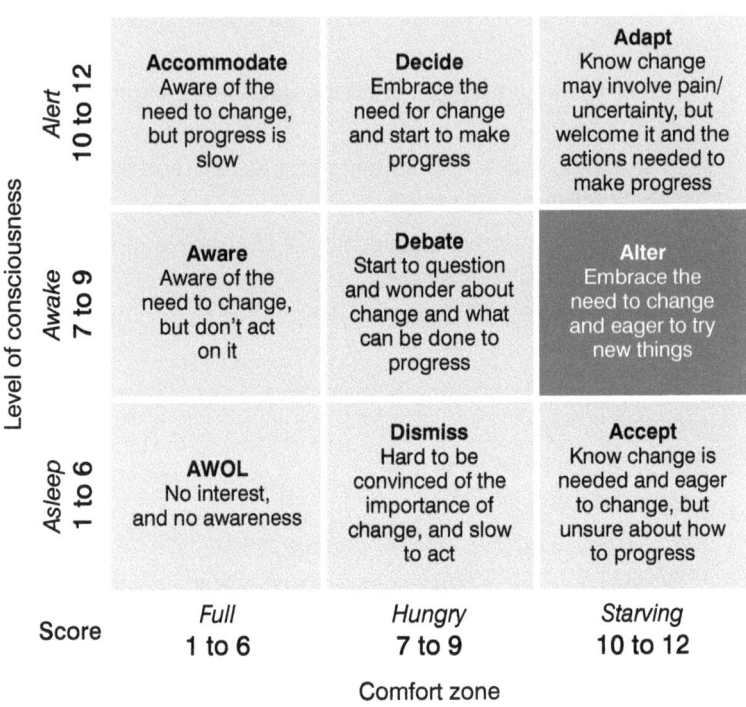

Figure 7: Example – assessing your personal position

These questions can act as triggers to get you thinking; thinking about how you may be approaching personal change at this point in your life. It is only by thinking and reflecting that you can recognise and understand what may need to change in yourself.

Importantly, these are not static emotions and they can change based on circumstances and timing. If you've faced a barrage of change it can become overwhelming and exhausting. Little wonder, in those circumstances, you may find yourself 'over it'. You want no change at all, regardless of your usual comfort zone and risk appetite.

To change means to do something different, to learn something new, to become something different. There are many types and degrees of change. What is common is that all change involves understanding and acceptance; a level of risk; a willingness to move out of your comfort zone; and a learning process where you try new things and do things differently.

Of course, moving through these stages – say from 'aware' to 'adapt' – isn't simple. That's because it involves you changing. Change often makes people feel uncomfortable. That's a good thing. If you are not feeling some form of discomfort then you aren't changing.

The mindset you take into any form of change is critical. Looking back to Figure 1 (page 7), is your mindset closed or empowered?

If you know your mindset and its operational levers it's easier to move forward and embrace change. You'll be able to build capabilities that extend your comfort zone so you can approach the change with confidence and determination.

Change is not linear. It's not always about putting one foot in front of the other. Sometimes there are stumbles and detours. Sometimes you may feel lost. However, it is important to keep focused on the direction you want to head in and have your eyes on your future and goals. From there, you'll be able to better face the challenges of change head on, and make strong and lasting headway.

More than 50 years ago, in one of the first of the big selling self-help books, David Schwartz wrote: *"Believe Big. The size of your success is determined by the size of your belief."*[3]

He goes on to say that if you set yourself small goals you can expect small achievements. If your goals are big you will achieve big things.

This still holds true today. Although success requires more than just thinking. You also need to operationalise it. To do that you'll want to understand how your mindset operates, its strengths and what may be holding you back. Remember, if you are not capable of change you can't expect those around you to change.

EVOLVE YOUR MINDSET

> "Between stimulus and response, there is a space. In that space lies our freedom and our power to choose our response. In our response lies our growth and our happiness."
>
> —*Viktor Frankl, Psychiatrist and Holocaust Survivor*

There is a famous Native American story, which goes like this…

One evening, an old Cherokee tells his grandson that inside all people a battle goes on between two wolves. One wolf is negativity: anger, sadness, stress, contempt, disgust, fear, embarrassment, guilt, shame and hate. The other is positivity: joy, gratitude, serenity, hope, pride, amusement, inspiration, awe and love.

The grandson thinks about this for a moment and then asks his grandfather, "Which wolf wins?"

The grandfather replies, "The one you feed."

So my question to you is: which wolf are you feeding?

Once you start to understand your mindset and how it's operating, you can start to take action to alter your mindset so it is more willing to embrace personal change.

Remember – this is about setting you up so that you can be your best self in your personal and professional life. To do that you need to be ready, willing and able to change how you think, which ultimately drives how you feel and act. And you need to shift and shape the perspectives that you hold, and be open to new possibilities and willing to try different practices.

Don't get discouraged as you work through these next elements. These learnings and practices are life skills. You will practise, refine and reflect on them for the rest of your life.

There are three primary steps in this process, and a number of practices that help you implement those steps (see Figure 8):

1. Choosing your paradigm
2. Exploring the possibilities
3. Taking action with practice.

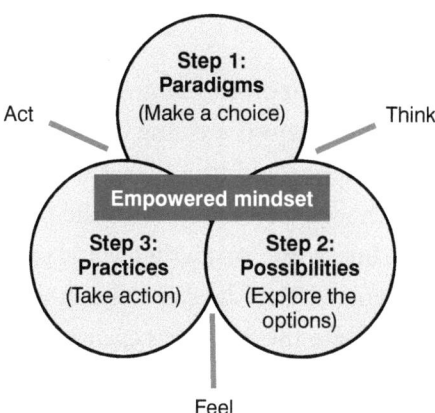

Figure 8: The three P's of an Empowered Mindset

The practices naturally overlap across each of these steps, and so you will find the practices listed as part of Step Three.

STEP ONE: Choose your paradigm

Paradigms are theories or groups of ideas that you hold about things. They are useful as they help you group common elements and frame issues. They can also hold you back, particularly if the paradigms are dated. The world moves on – all the time – and therefore it's necessary to change your paradigms accordingly.

This is not about throwing away everything you know or understand. Instead, it's about being open to new ideas and being willing to be challenged and accept that perhaps your ideas are no longer helping you be the best you can be. It's about leveraging your strengths, and knowing your purpose and the principles by which you live your life. It's about not letting single events define you.

Instead you can choose your response to life's events and select the meaning you put around those events. It's about not letting yourself be bound by convention or expectations as to who you should be.

It's your life. You get to write the narrative. What stories are running in your head about who you are and what you can be? These stories you tell yourself, and the stories that others tell you, shape your paradigms.

The story goes that Napoleon was given a star sapphire stone by his grandmother when he was a young boy growing up in Corsica (Italy). His grandmother told him that it would bring him good fortune because whoever had the stone would become Emperor of France. Now for a boy from Corsica that would seem like a long way to travel. It's reported that he kept the stone his whole life. Apparently on his death the stone was examined and it turned out to be a fake. Fake or otherwise, it didn't matter. It was a useful talisman for Napoleon because as you know he became the Emperor of France.

How do you respond in the face of adversity?

Do you throw your hands up in despair or over-dramatise the situation? Or are you calm and deliberate and able to bounce back quickly?

Resilience is a very powerful characteristic which is based on a paradigm that says "I can move forward from this". It's the ability to withstand stress and adversity. Being resilient doesn't mean you ignore how you feel or that you don't experience stress, sadness or hurt. It's about how you respond to it. People who are resilient have a way of recognising the issue, reframing what it means and adapting to the changed circumstances.

A very personal example for me is when I found out that my husband and I could never have children. I am lucky. I was born an optimist and I've always been able to find ways to position things and look for the positive. This situation was harder. I still remember when we went to the christening of our godchild, getting in the car after the service and both of us bursting into tears. We were delighted to be godparents but there was an ache in our hearts for the child we would never have. To cope, we repurposed our life. We looked at all the things we could do more easily because we didn't have children. These included travel (which we love); helping our nieces and nephews; and also supporting the needs of children overseas. This really helped. I also knew that rationally there was no point in getting fixated on something that was outside our control. It was time to regroup and move forward with our lives together.

In today's ever-changing world, resilience is a really important skill to have in your toolkit. None of us can alter the pace of change. So we need to be equipped to face it, and thrive through it. The famous Roman Emperor, Marcus Aurelius, understood the power of resilience and that we all have a choice to make about how we respond to events.

He said: *"If you are distressed by anything external, the pain is not due to the thing itself but to your estimate of it; and this you have the power to revoke at any moment".*

This is a very powerful expression. It goes to the heart of the fact that whatever happens in life, even if it feels like there is no control, there are still elements that you can control. This belief in self-determination is a fundamental factor in people who live happy and fulfilled lives.

Marcus Aurelius was also a stoic philosopher. The word stoic is used today and is usually associated with people who keep a 'stiff upper lip' or don't show emotions in the face of adversity. As a school of philosophy it dates back to the third century, BC. Stoics based their approach to life on being in tune with nature and guided by virtue. Through their ethics-based approach they saw everything that was external to the person (i.e. suffering, happiness, poverty, wealth, etc.) as all equally unimportant. What was important was how the person lived their life. They also practised a technique called the premeditation of evils. It sounds worse than it is. It involves thinking about what's the worst thing that could happen as a result of a situation. What the technique often reveals is that it's never as bad as you think it is.

I was mentoring an executive who was facing extreme stress at work. She had a boss who she felt she couldn't communicate with. She also felt that they had a bad relationship and he didn't value her work effort. I asked her whether she had broached the subject with him. She hadn't. I then got her to do this exercise: to write down a list of the worst things that could happen if she was to have a conversation with her boss about how they worked together. At the top of the list was that he might get angry with her and not renew her contract. We talked that through. The interesting point was she didn't want her contract to be renewed anyway. So what she saw as the worst thing might not have been all that bad were it to happen. It provided her with enormous relief. She also went on to have a great conversation with him; finding out that her perspective on the relationship was quite different to his.

So next time you are facing a dilemma or crisis ask yourself: what's the worst thing that could possibly happen if I do this?

Rather than see challenging situations as a negative, embrace the learnings, perspective and resilience that comes from the experience. Ultimately, how you choose to respond will have a major impact on how you come through the other side and whether you just survive it or whether it defines you in a positive way.

Doing this is about resetting your internal programming to believe in your self-mastery and free will. It's critical to uncover the paradigms and assumptions that are currently running or limiting your life. Understand where they come from and when they are triggered.

The brilliant science of neuroplasticity has proven that you can rewire your brain. Education, doing new things and undertaking meditation creates new neural pathways, and increases the number of branches among neurons (i.e. how your synapses fire up). For example, people who meditate have been found to have a thicker insula (i.e. that part of the brain which is activated when you pay close attention to something). While the size of a London taxi driver's hippocampus (the area of the brain that stores spatial data) increases the more time he or she spends as a taxi driver.

It's common practice to use the metaphor of your brain as a muscle. It's very apt as the more you exercise the healthier you get. So too, the more you exercise your brain the healthier it gets. In fact, as you do new things you are rewiring your brain. How amazing is that! And the science shows we are never too old to learn new things.

You can choose how you wire your brain. Techniques such as mindfulness – where you pause, breath, reflect and then respond – can help in this regard.

STEP TWO: Explore the possibilities

Every day we are presented with options and possibilities. They exist around every corner. Do you know which ones to take and which ones to avoid? Do you even see the possibilities in front of you?

Possibilities are amazing, but they can also be intimidating. Taking advantage of possibilities is about being curious and open to what is in front of you. And at the same time accepting that you don't always know where the possibility may take you. It's about being prepared to open doors for yourself, rather than waiting for someone to open the door for you. Once you've opened the door, it's time to explore and take a leap into the unknown. The more you practise this, the easier it will become.

I remember as a young girl reading the book about Helen Keller.

Born in 1880, a childhood illness left her deaf and blind, and her world closed in as she was unable to communicate. Through her teacher, Anne Sullivan, she was able to learn how to communicate and her world re-opened. It was transformative. She became a well-respected author and political activist, and she gained great perspective on how to look at the world and what happens when things don't go to plan. She said: *"When one door of happiness closes, another opens; but often we look so long at the closed door that we do not see the one which has been opened for us."*

Of course, she was talking about mindset. This closed door mentality means you close yourself off to possibilities and opportunities. However, this often occurs subconsciously. It's almost like the responsibility has been outsourced to someone else. Outsourcing can be fabulously productive and liberating. By outsourcing you get other people to do the things that aren't your core focus. It frees you to spend your time on what you do best. However, you shouldn't outsource everything. And top of the list is your ability to choose the things that matter. Being able to choose and knowing that you can choose is a critical part of having a healthy mindset

Stephen Covey in his book, *The 7 Habits of Highly Effective People*, talks about the Circle of Concern and Circle of Influence.[4] We can be concerned about things which we can't influence. But, we should spend our time and energy on those ideas, issues and opportunities we can influence. Effective people know the difference. They know that it's a waste of time to focus their efforts trying to change things over which they have no control.

You can be concerned about the fact that it is raining and going to ruin your outdoor party, but you can't change it. What you can change is the venue for the party or what you wear. It is much wiser to spend your energy on what you can influence.

In life, you'll meet people who let the little things drag them down. They are always complaining about something. They seem to suck the energy from those around them. Their unhappiness permeates everything they do. They don't know how to make the most out of their life.

In contrast, I've met some people who seemingly have very little and they are incredibly positive about their life. They are able to keep things in perspective and see the possibilities in difficult situations.

My husband has amazing perspective and insight. If I'm complaining about something he can make me see the other side. He doesn't let little things bother him.

We have a very comfortable and well equipped three bedroom house. The third bedroom is my office but the house still has plenty of space. I like my space and I can be quite particular about how things are done. One time we were faced with both my parents and my brother (and his girlfriend) wanting to visit at the same time. From my perspective, the house would have felt way too crowded and we would have needed to have my brother and his girlfriend sleep on the floor. My solution was to suggest they stay at a hotel.

My husband was bemused because from his perspective the house was huge as he was used to having lots of people in confined spaces. Craig grew up in India and he has a completely different concept of space. As he jokingly said: "Michelle, don't be ridiculous. In India we'd have 11 people sleeping in the space the size of our laundry". Now he was exaggerating but the point was well made. I was letting my expectations get in the way of my relationship with my brother. I was complaining about something that was irrelevant and petty. In this case, I could control both the situation and how I was responding to it.

Nelson Mandela, in his autobiography, *The Long Walk to Freedom* said that he was fundamentally an optimist but he wasn't sure whether that came from nature or nurture. He wrote: *"Part of being optimistic is keeping one's head pointed towards the sun, one's feet moving forward. There were many dark moments when my faith in humanity was sorely tested, but I would not and could not give myself up to despair*".[5]

Nelson Mandela was the perfect example of this principle in action. He knew he couldn't control what would happen to him every day. But, he could choose how he responded. He could choose his mindset and his reactions.

When you don't make a conscious choice you have, by default, outsourced the choice to another person or situation. Applying a conscious choice is about being alert to how you think, clear on where you focus your attention and selective as to how you subsequently respond.

This is not about denial. It's about being realistic about what's in front of you. It's about how you face challenges and how you respond to situations. Do you put your head in the sand and hope they go away? Or do you face them front on? Do you look to turn challenges into opportunities?

STEP THREE: Take action with practice

The saying goes that "practice makes perfect". Striving for perfection can be dangerous, but practising and being willing to learn and grow isn't dangerous. Changing your mindset won't happen overnight. It requires constant vigilance and effort.

Focusing on the practices below will help put you in the best possible position to deal with what is going on around you.

Practice One: Mindfulness meditation

Mindfulness has been a buzz word in recent times. Everywhere you turn there are books and articles spelling out why it's good for you. Devotees swear to its health, lifestyle and relationship benefits. Opponents dismiss it as another fad.

Mindfulness has been around for centuries. It's an ancient practice dating back to early Buddhist teachings. Today's mindfulness-based interventions are derived from those early learnings. A modern-day mindfulness expert, Jon Kabat-Zinn, defines it as: *"The awareness that arises from paying attention, on purpose, in the present moment, without judgment"*.[6]

In this state there are various levels of progress:

- Level 1 – focuses on being present to what is happening by being aware and curious
- Level 2 – focuses on bringing understanding to what is happening by being open and accepting
- Level 3 – focuses on responding to the issue by being kind to yourself and others.

Each level involves being conscious of what is happening, rather than responding reactively and subconsciously. When you are going through a change or a stressful event, either at a personal or organisational level, invariably things will go wrong. This gives rise to doubt – creating feelings of stress, tension and discomfort. This all happens automatically. As soon as our brain detects a threat, a series of things start to happen (see Figure 9):

Figure 9: Reactions to stress

Stress triggers detected by sensory systems in the amygdala
↓
Hypothalamus sends signal to adrenal glands
↓
Fight or flight response: + Adrenalin + Cortisol + Norepinephrine released
↓
Body responds: heart rate, breathing
Emotional reaction: outburst
Thoughts: anger, victim, blame

When stress is detected by the brain's amygdala it sends a message to the hypothalamus which in turn triggers the adrenal glands to release adrenalin, cortisol and norepinephrine. This chemical surge stimulates your 'flight or fight responses'. You will feel it in your body as your heart starts to race or your breathing becomes more rapid. It will also play out in your behaviour as when you are stressed your pre-frontal cortex is less active.

All of this happens in less than a fifth of a second. These responses are necessary to protect us. However, if they are constantly activated they can have very negative health consequences.

This is eloquently expressed by Dr Bruce Lipton in his book *The Biology of Belief*, where he explains the impact that arises when stress hormones are released into the blood stream.[7] Blood that was previously nourishing our visceral organs is forced to nourish the tissues of our limbs – providing energy to escape the situation. The visceral organs include vital organs such as the heart, liver and kidney. When these organs stop receiving blood they stop functioning. That means they stop performing things like: digestion, excretion and all the other essential functions that you need them to do for you to function. Your body, when it is in fight or flight mode, represses your immune system to conserve energy. That's why you get sick when you are stressed.

Lipton goes on to explain: This *"... system is a brilliant mechanism for handling acute stresses. However, this protection system was not designed to be continuously activated".*[8]

In today's chaotic and busy world, you face many daily triggers that can set this system off. These are not situations that threaten your survival, they are just the daily stresses of modern-day living. What happens is that the system is overly activated causing elevated stress levels, often at chronic levels. That's why learning to meditate and practise mindfulness is essential. The choice you make about how you respond to events will either minimise stressful feelings or exacerbate them. Mindfulness can help because the more you practise the art the better you'll be able to manage how you feel, think and act in any given moment.

Think of it like this…

There's a trigger which may be someone telling you something you didn't want to hear. For example, the person hasn't agreed with your suggestion at work. Don't just react to it.

Instead… Stop and breathe. Notice your immediate reaction and what you want to say in response to the trigger. Notice how you are feeling. Reflect on the underlying reasons for those reactions and feelings. And then, and only then, respond.

This little exercise can be done quickly. And the more you practise it – the better you'll become at it.

Over time, you'll find you will be more aware of what is happening around you. You'll also be more conscious of what triggers set you off, and what you need to do to maintain perspective in the face of uncertainty, ambiguity and complexity. This means you'll be able to react to negative news more calmly and objectively – creating a better frame of mind to determine the best way to move forward.

You can also practise this at various points during the day. Years ago I was taught a five-minute, breath-awareness exercise by a yoga instructor. The idea was to use this activity at various points during the day: on the bus on the way home, before going to an important meeting or when I was feeling stressed.

It works like this…

Find a comfortable and quiet place to sit.
Close your eyes.
Become aware of your breathing.
Notice its depth and how your stomach rises and falls.
Try to breathe slowly and deeply. Breathe in through your nose and out through your nose.

As your mind wanders, come back to the breathing.
Keep doing this for five minutes.
Open your eyes.
Get back to your day.

It's amazing how relaxed you'll feel after a short period of time.

I used to think that I could never find the time to practise meditation. When I understood its power and benefits I moved it up the priority scale. I start each day doing a short 10-minute mindfulness meditation practice. It's pretty hard to say that you can't find 10 minutes.

I was given this advice by a mindfulness instructor and it made all the difference. Before that time I'd been trying to find space for a 30-minute practice. It just never happened. I didn't have 30 minutes, but I found I had 10. All I did was turn the clock 15 minutes to the right. That's right – I got up 15 minutes earlier every day so I could do this. Eventually it became a habit that I looked forward to.

Practice Two: Open your mind

If you want to expand your possibilities, build your resilience and thrive through change it will help if you are open and willing to:

1. Be curious and have an open mind – investigating issues through multiple lenses helps you see things from many perspectives. This, in turn, helps you realise that your negative view of the event may not be the reality.
2. Surround yourself with people who will challenge, inspire and support you, and be accepting of others and accepting of difference.
3. Manage stress – practising mindfulness will help, as will exercising often, eating well, meditating and laughing lots.
4. Take time to reflect each day – examining what happened

and how you responded. It is only through reflection that you'll be able to understand your trigger points, and how you can better manage them.

5. Use your energy wisely – don't waste your time on things that are outside your control.
6. Learn from your mistakes – view mistakes as an opportunity to experiment, learn and grow, rather than viewing them as a failure. All growth involves mistakes, pain and learning.
7. Quieten your inner voice – all of us have an inner voice that can be an unharnessed critic. This voice is often trying to protect us. Understand its message of protection, but don't let it hold you back. Reflect and be open to new ideas.
8. Feed your mind with healthy thoughts, and nourish it with new information and experiences.
9. Don't expect life to be easy – there are always ups and downs.
10. Continue to push the boundaries of your expectations throughout your life. Don't let other people's expectations define you or hem you in.

When you are open to the possibilities and to your responsibility to choose from those possibilities, a whole new world of opportunity arises. This is more than just the 'believe and you will succeed' mantra. To be successful you have to take action. And that's about practice.

Practice Three: Upskill your set point for happiness

Aristotle said: *"Happiness is the meaning and the purpose of life, the whole aim and end of human existence".*

We all have a set point for happiness. Think of it like a scale. Just as everybody weighs a certain amount, every person has a happiness level they typically operate at. That set point remains relatively constant. There are things that will temporarily adjust it. For example, a new job, winning the lottery, or buying a new car will temporarily make a person happier. Sadly, these are only short-term activators. They don't last.

In today's society, people equate money and success with happiness. This is a fallacy. In fact, 90% of happiness is based on your internal mental view of the world and how your brain processes what is happening around you.

Research shows that genetics accounts for about 50% of your happiness quota (i.e. your happiness setting at birth, predisposition and personality traits); 10% is due to circumstances; and the remaining 40% to variants that you can determine; that is, intentional activity that you undertake.[9]

In this case, the researchers defined intentional to mean "discrete actions or practices in which people can choose to engage". These are activities that require some form of effort.

Now you might be sitting back and thinking that's really interesting but why should I care? You should care because how happy you are impacts your life and likelihood of success.

Lyubomirsky, King and Diener examined whether happiness leads to success, and the causal factors. They argued that the happiness–success link exists not only because success makes people happy but, more importantly, because having a positive disposition engenders success. Their results showed that happiness is associated with and "precedes numerous successful outcomes, as well as behaviours paralleling success".[10]

The researchers also reviewed data which showed that happy individuals are more likely than their less happy peers to have fulfilling marriages and relationships, high incomes, superior work performance, community involvement, robust health and a long life.

The happier you are the more likely you are to experience success. They found that happiness has a compounding effect, because happiness, which has its origins in personality and past successes, leads to behaviours that in turn lead to future success.

When you are with people who are happy they build you up, not drag you down. Their happiness is usually infectious. You can feel their energy. There's no doubt that happier people have higher levels of resilience.

I'm lucky. I was born with a relatively high set point for happiness. I've always had the ability to reframe situations, and to see the learnings when things go wrong. That doesn't mean I don't feel pain or experience sadness, but I've always been able to find learnings and positive outcomes…on reflection.

Many years ago I worked with a senior leader. He wasn't the easiest person to work with. He had a big ego and saw himself as incredibly important. He also held a position of power in the organisation. I didn't enjoy working with him, but I could see the long-term benefits for my career so I stuck it out. I got to the point where I knew there was nothing more to learn from working in this role. It was time to move on. When I told him – as diplomatically as I could – that I wanted to find a new role, he responded by saying he didn't want me going anywhere, as that didn't suit him.

He proceeded to block career moves I tried to make in the organisation. It was a pretty traumatic time for me. I felt stymied and didn't know what to do. I sought advice as to my best course of action. Over time, the situation was resolved and I moved on and up.

However, despite the horrible nature of what was going on I was always able to look back and reflect on what I learnt from my time working with him. I also knew that my career wouldn't be where it is today if I hadn't worked with him. I gained enormous experience and connections from the role.

My point is, often people think that happiness is about being happy all the time. It's not. It's about recognising there will always be ups and downs but you can't let the downs drag you down.

You can choose to put in place practices to make yourself happier. It's like a plant. For it to thrive it needs to be nourished, watered and cared for. So too for your happiness quotient.

If you want to change your setting for happiness it is wise to take deliberate and planned action. Consider including activities such as these in your day:

1. Craft a gratitude mantra that you say every day. Expressing gratitude helps you feel happier and builds your resilience. When you look at what you have vis-à-vis others you can see how much you have to be thankful for.

2. As part of this practice, focus on one to three things to be thankful for every day. This can be as simple as – the sun was shining or I had a great cup of coffee. Buy a journal and carry it with you. Write those positive experiences in your journal. Do this daily. Writing down your experiences helps your brain relive the event, and so you get the brain's feel-good chemicals released into your blood stream.

3. Spend time connecting with nature. Appreciate the grace and beauty of what is around you every day in the natural environment. Take the time to pause. This can be a five minute pause. Look around you. What do you notice? What do you feel? Connect your feelings with your environment.

4. Exercise and meditate regularly. Build a routine so these activities are mapped out in advance and scheduled in your calendar. Exercise and meditation are as important as eating and sleeping.

5. Get eight hours sleep a night. Sleep is restorative and your brain can't function without it. It's hard to be focused, mindful and reflective when you're tired.
6. Eat well and drink lots of water to stay hydrated.
7. Do nice things for other people. When you do something nice for someone else it makes you feel good. Helping others helps you realise the positive forces in your life that others may not have.
8. Wish people well – if you are in a busy environment take a moment to stop and notice those around you. Internally cultivate the wish that you want them to be happy, healthy and free of suffering. Wishing others well is good for your own emotional state.
9. Devote time to important relationships every single day. This goes beyond maintaining connections on social media. Ring people. Have a coffee with them. Send someone a hand-written note. The connection needs to be personal. Close bonds and being comfortable to share how you feel, and being open about experiences is healthy and very good for the soul. People who are happy have strong connections to the community and good friends.
10. Accept yourself and love yourself for your flaws. No one is perfect. Everyone is still learning and evolving. To do this you need to be open to learning and making mistakes.
11. Strive to find purpose and meaning in your life – people with purpose are generally happier and more resilient as they are clear about their goals and where they are heading in life. Set short, medium and long-term goals – each with the right amount of stretch and do-ability.

Building the foundation for an empowered mindset takes time and effort. Identify the paradigms that underpin your mindset. Be open to new possibilities. Make a conscious choice to implement these three practices. These practices are skills for life.

3. Strengthen your integrity

> "The thought manifests as the word
> The word manifests as the deed
> The deed develops into habit
> And habit hardens into character
> So watch the thought and its ways with care,
> And let it spring from love born out of concern
> for all beings…
> As the shadow follows the body
> As we think so we become."
>
> —*Buddha, in the Dharmapadda*

The saying goes that it takes a lifetime to build a reputation, and seconds to destroy it. The foundation of your reputation is integrity. A person with integrity lives their life according to moral and ethical principles. At a practical level, your integrity is about what you say and do every day, the decisions you make and how you treat people.

People would bristle if they heard that their integrity was being questioned. For most people their integrity is valued, and not something they would want to lose. However, your integrity can become tarnished and eroded slowly, over time, if you're not careful.

Dan Ariely, a professor of psychology and behavioural economics, talks about the fact that everyone lies a little bit. *"We like to believe that a few bad apples spoil the virtuous bunch. But, research shows that everyone cheats a little – right up to the point where they lose their sense of integrity."* [11]

He goes on to talk about the research that he and his colleagues have undertaken over the last 10 years. They've used experiments and reviewed data from insurance claims to employment histories. What they found certainly surprised me. They found that *"Everybody has the capacity to be dishonest, and almost everybody cheats – just by a little."*

Ariely concedes that while there are a few exceptions, the vast majority of people are driven to cheating because they want to gain the benefit they will get from it – *"the money or the glory".* And yet, they still want to regard themselves as *"honest, honourable people".*

I find that explanation a little too depressing, and I'd rather believe that not everyone is motivated by money alone. That said, it is true that we are not always as ethical as we may think we are. This is because we often make decisions subconsciously and are not aware of the biases built into our decision-making process. The environment or culture in which we live and work plays a big part in the nature and scale of those biases. An organisational culture that tolerates or encourages behaviour that is 'dodgy' can see people behave in ways that are out of character. Behaviour that they wouldn't consider appropriate or ethical is adopted as they become 'culturalised' to the accepted way of behaving in that environment.

>  **STEP UP TIP**
>
> Ask yourself regularly:
>
> How am I showing up every day? Am I acting with integrity? Is my behaviour congruent with my stated values?
>
> If it's inconsistent, you will be sending mixed messages to people working with you and your integrity will be at risk.

In psychology, the terms 'espoused values' and 'values in use' are used. These terms were coined by Argyris and Schon back in 1974. Our espoused values are the values we talk about. We might say that we value honesty. Yet, if we are given an honest answer to a question such as "Have I put on weight?", and the answer is "Yes" we may not be happy with the response. Our response is our values in use. Our values in use are the values that we use every day when we do things. For example, we might say we value the environment but not recycle or do anything to improve the planet's health.

As those examples show there can be conflict and a gap between our espoused values and values in use.

History is littered with examples of people who were blind to the environment they worked in and the dangers it posed, and didn't have the courage to protect their integrity. In the end, they became captured by the situation and their integrity was sold. A prime example was the senior executives at Enron, most particularly the CEO and CFO. It also filtered down to many of the traders on the trading floor who bought and sold energy trades. The manipulation of energy during California's energy crisis (2000 to 2001) is well documented. Motivated by money, certain energy traders quite happily manipulated the system for the organisation's and ultimately their own personal gain (as they benefitted from the company's bonus scheme). Thousands of words have been written about Enron's culture and the consequential impact it had on the behaviour of people who worked there. In this culture, they were rewarded for their pursuit of a profit at-all-costs approach, and to behave otherwise was unacceptable.[12]

Another famous example is the case of the Ford Pinto. This too has been well documented. The Ford Pinto was a very popular two door, compact car that sold well in the United States. It had a major design flaw though – the fuel tank was in the back of the car, and if a car was rear-ended it could burst into flames. The company knew that the design of the car was causing deaths. They undertook a cost benefit analysis, which showed that it was cheaper to deal with the law suits from the deaths than to change the car's design. This was recorded in an internal memo, which highlighted the cost of reinforcing the car's rear-end ($121 million) versus the potential payout to victims ($50 million).[13] In the now infamous report, Ford often referred to "dead injured persons" as "units".

I've seen people in organisations who considered themselves ethical and having high integrity do things that other people would easily view as unethical. Often the unravelling of a person's integrity takes place little by little. A small cheat on a work expense claim which goes unnoticed gets larger over time.

In one organisation I worked in, despite the expense policy clearly showing that gifts for staff were not permitted, the leaders regularly bought Christmas gifts for staff on the corporate card. I paid for the gifts for my team at my own expense. Part of my reason for doing this is that I couldn't say the gift was from me if I hadn't paid for it. My peers saw nothing wrong with their behaviour. In some respects they were right because that was just the way things were done, but it was against company policy.

At the other end of the spectrum, there are people who are conscious of their environment and who have the courage to remain centred and true to their principles. I've worked with leaders like this who operated with integrity and good intent. This created space and support for their team to be the best they could be.

Maintaining integrity encompasses two core attributes: having the courage to think and act, and also being conscious of the environment or situation you are in. Both attributes have a range. For courage you can think about it in terms of 'absent' at one end and 'present' at the other end. While your consciousness is either 'active' or 'passive'. How each attribute is activated will have consequences (either positive or negative) for your integrity (see Figure 10).

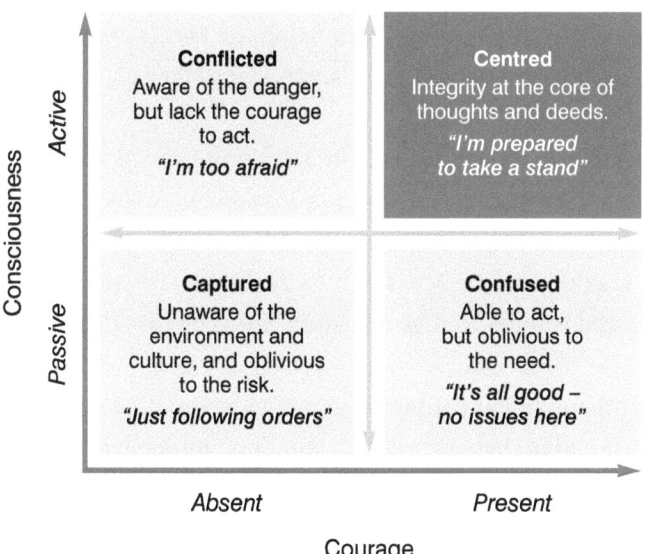

Figure 10: The maintaining integrity model

These are important dimensions to consider. If you have no courage and are completely unaware of environmental influences you are captured by what is going on around you and are very open to putting your integrity at risk. This is the person who goes around oblivious to what is really going on. If you fall into this trap, you ultimately end up becoming complicit with bad behaviour when things go wrong. People in this category often say "I was just following orders". But, as history shows, following orders is never a good defence.

If you're conscious of what is going on but don't have the courage to act on it you become conflicted. This is a terrible position to be in. The stress levels are enormous. You know what is happening is wrong. You know there is something that should be done, but you don't have the courage to take action.

Social psychologist Leon Festinger published his theory of cognitive dissonance in 1957.[14] It explained the distressing mental state that arises when people find their beliefs are inconsistent with their actions. People in this state strive to bring the two into balance – and often it is their beliefs that will change, and so they end up being trapped by the environment.

Without over-dramatising, reaching this point can be likened to the character Dr Faustus in Christopher Marlowe's late 16th century play of the same name. Dr Faustus sold his soul to the devil for power. It was not until he was about to die that he began to regret his actions and wanted to make amends. Sadly, by that time it was too late.

On the other hand, if courage is present, but you have no awareness you just end up being confused. You don't understand what is concerning people or why they are worried about what is happening. You have the ability to take action, but you don't know what needs to be done. You are oblivious to the situation and so ineffective in securing change.

You become centred when you have the balance of both courage and consciousness. This isn't always easy, because maintaining integrity comes with risks and challenges. There are plenty of stories of people who have taken a stand in the face of enormous pressure and have faced backlash as a result. It often takes a huge personal toll. Interestingly, though, if they're asked about whether they would do it again invariably the answer is "Yes".

In the 1980s, Jeffrey Wigand, a former Vice President of a United States-based tobacco company went public with inside knowledge that tobacco companies had tried to conceal the dangers of smoking for years.[15] His view was that he was clear on what and why he took a stand. *"The word whistle-blower suggests that you're a tattletale or that you're somehow disloyal,"* he said. *"But I wasn't disloyal in the least bit. People were dying. I was loyal to a higher order of ethical responsibility."*[16] This extracted a considerable personal toll; with impacts on his personal and family life, and professional reputation.

When you know the right thing to do and you do nothing it eats away at your moral fibre. It's like a rotten apple. If the core is bad – it permeates throughout the whole.

At a broader level, if you're a leader your actions will be noticed and emulated. This plays out all the time in organisations. If the person leading the organisation is unethical, this filters through to how business gets done in that organisation. It's therefore critical to know what you need to do to stay true to yourself and to ensure your moral compass is pointed in the right direction.

I remember from an early age being told that if you are ever confused about a course of action and what is the right thing to do, you can use the newspaper test as a way of reflecting. Ask yourself: what would happen if your family or friends read about what you have done? How would you feel? Knowing that your decision or action could become public often helps you make a good decision.

Alternatively, ask yourself the question that Benjamin Franklin asked himself everyday: *"What good shall I do today?"* and his evening question – *"What good have I done today?"*

What would your answer be?

UNPLUG YOUR BIAS

> "Organisms organise, and what human organisms organise is meaning".
>
> —William Perry, Psychologist

If you want to be more effective and stay true to your integrity, you need to start by accepting the fact that you're biased and therefore you can be blind to the obvious.

Psychologists Dan Simons and Christopher Chabris conducted an experiment involving two teams.[17] One team was wearing white shirts and the other team was wearing black shirts. The teams were filmed and this was played back to a group of people. They were instructed to count the number of times the ball was passed between the players wearing the white shirts, and to ignore the team in black shirts. Halfway through the video a person wearing a gorilla suit appeared – thumped their chest – and moved off screen. The gorilla's on the screen for just under 10 seconds – not a long time – but still long enough to think that people would notice.

When the researchers asked the people to say how many times the ball was thrown they got the number right. However, when they were asked about the gorilla about half the people watching the film had failed to see it. How was that possible? It turns out that the instructions to count and ignore the other team caused the brain to focus solely on that – to the exclusion of other things going on around it.

Not only are you biased but your brain can selectively ignore vital pieces of information.

The good news is you're not alone. Everyone has bias, much of which is subconscious. The trouble is that this subconscious bias can get in the way of a good decision being made. When that happens you subconsciously lose your perspective. You're no longer centred and your integrity can be called into question.

Think of it like this. Your integrity is the compass that helps to guide you. However, if one of the elements in the compass is faulty, you will head in the wrong direction. If you don't know that the elements are faulty you can easily go on the wrong path and end up at the wrong destination. At which point you'll be confused or lost.

How do you create the most effective level of consciousness and courage so you remain centred and your integrity continues to guide you in the right direction? How does your bias become minimised or neutralised? It's about having the right level of awareness, analysis and aptitude (see Figure 11 overleaf).

Awareness

It's important to understand the level of consciousness you have about the decisions you are making, and the bias that may be influencing your decision-making.

Consider:

- Are you aware of your bias preferences?
- Are you conscious of the limitations or bias that may be constraining how you think?
- Are you on the look-out for influencing factors that affect how you are processing information?

Analysis

This is about how you analyse yourself and accept yourself for who you are, how you seek out information sources, and ensure you are not stacking the decks in favour of your own world view.

Scrutinise:

- Is the problem you are trying to solve clear?
- Are you willing to take risks and back yourself, or are you easily swayed by the opinions of others?

- How much information are you looking at? Is it a case of information overload?
- Are you seeking views from a range of diverse sources and considering the outliers or silent minority?
- Are you devoting the right amount of time to the decision and including time for reflection?

Aptitude

Aptitude is your willingness to challenge assumptions and pre-conceived ideas and to take on different ideas and opinions.

Examine:

- Are you willing to learn from your mistakes?
- Are you tired when making the decision, or too stressed and unable to focus?
- Are you taking care of yourself and putting yourself in the best position to make decisions?
- Are you finding ways to filter out bias-laden decisions?
- Are your purpose and intent clear?

Figure 11: The strengthened integrity model

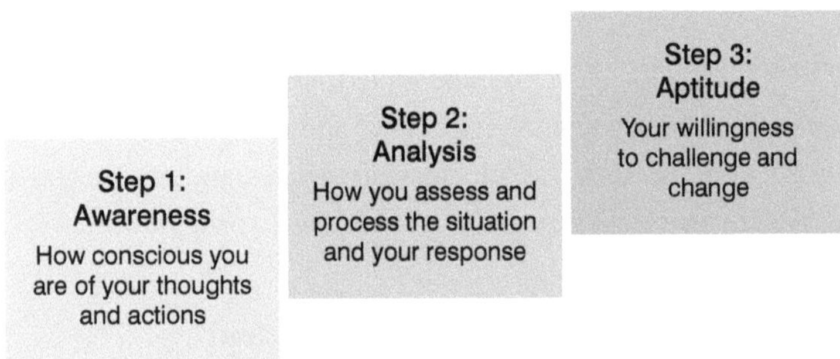

Step 1: Awareness
How conscious you are of your thoughts and actions

Step 2: Analysis
How you assess and process the situation and your response

Step 3: Aptitude
Your willingness to challenge and change

STEP ONE: Elevate your awareness

The first step in unplugging your bias is to elevate your awareness of the bias that exists.

Your brain loves bias. No doubt you think you're a highly rational being and that this rationality extends to how you make decisions. Unfortunately, it's not the case. Bias pervades decision-making because decisions aren't made on facts alone. They're made on hunches, feelings, past experiences and gut reactions.

But, you're not alone. It affects everyone. These biases are due to the way our brain makes decisions, and to conditioning. In the earlier discussion on mindset, I talked about how your mindset is shaped by your experiences. Those experiences, over time, shape how you think and act and they can become fixed. You interpret the world through your lens of past experience. Your past experience has taught you that certain things will happen in certain ways. It is these expectations that create assumptions. Your assumptions cause you to filter out information that doesn't fit with your world view, and instead you actively seek information that does. These become blind spots, which are often at the root of differences of opinion and bad relationships.

This is your brain at work.

Your brain can be likened to a pattern-recognition machine, and a massive filing system that likes to sort and categorise things. But, your brain has limitations. The pre-frontal cortex, which is the part of the brain that is actively engaged when you make decisions, has a limited amount of energy. Every time you make a decision energy is used, and so the brain finds ways to conserve energy. Similarly, your working memory has limited capacity, and so the brain has found ways to try and overcome this too.

Your brain is constantly and rapidly trying to make sense of the world and what is happening. To do that, and to ease the cognitive load this requires, it takes shortcuts. It compresses information and sorts it into patterns. By doing this it is making large tasks and complex issues easier to manage, and ultimately, remember (i.e. retrieve from the filing cabinet). Your brain is also very efficiently, but sometimes not all that helpfully, discarding information that doesn't fit with its world view.

So while your brain is seeing, retrieving, sorting and making sense of information it is always trying to do it in the most energy-efficient way. It takes energy and time to store information in the brain, and energy again to retrieve it. So, if the brain is trying to conserve energy it makes sense to try and find easier ways to do this. Without using predictive patterns or heuristics your brain would need to use dramatically more resources, putting a huge drain on the pre-frontal cortex, to process what is happening and what you should do in response.

Your brain likes to take the path of least resistance. This is where it gets dangerous because taking the path of least resistance means you will let expectations and assumptions drive how you think and act. Your bias will be out in full force – and your brain won't provide a warning signal.

Daniel Kahneman in his brilliant book *Thinking, Fast and Slow* shared his years of research into this field.[18] He explained the different modes of the brain's thought processes – labelling them System 1 and System 2. System 1 is the fast, instinctive, emotional and unconscious processing; while System 2 is slower, more deliberate, controlled and logical. It is the reliance on the automatic and instinctual part of the brain that leads to bias, as you place way too much confidence in your own judgment and opinions.

He explains, for example, the concept of 'anchoring'. This is a bias where people give disproportionate weight to the first information they receive. This can be an impression, a number, a fact, or a piece of data which impacts their subsequent thoughts and decisions. You will have heard the expression – "first impressions count". You may not have realised the statement's significance extends beyond how people look. In fact, anchoring plays out when people buy houses and cars, or are in salary negotiations. The first offer made usually anchors the rest of the discussion.

Studies using the Implicit Association test confirm the level of bias that exists in people. This test is used by social psychologists to measure implicit attitudes; that is, attitudes that a person may have that they may not be explicitly aware of. People taking the test are asked to make a split second decision based on word associations. In a particular example, participants are asked whether they have a positive or negative reaction to images of different types of people. At least 75% of people taking the test displayed bias. In this case, the bias was in favour of people who were young, rich and white. The study found that the mere desire to not be biased did not stop participants from being biased.[19]

So what type of cognitive biases exist? The ones that you will most commonly come across include:

- **Confirmation:** you ignore information that doesn't fit with your beliefs and actively look for evidence to support and back your position.
- **Anchoring:** as mentioned earlier this is where you base decisions on the earliest piece of information you receive, ignoring later pieces of information that may be more relevant or correct.
- **In group:** desire for acceptance and a need to be part of the 'in group' can cause you to conform and behave in a certain way due to the pressure of others.
- **Discounting:** the brain prefers rewards it can get now, and so you will sacrifice a bigger reward (that comes later) for a smaller reward (which you can get now).

- **Mere exposure:** you prefer things which are familiar, and so being exposed to something over time can make you like something more than you did initially.
- **Status quo:** preferring the familiar, you will actively defend and prefer the status quo and see it as better than alternatives.
- **Loss aversion:** the brain is wired to focus more on what you can lose then what you might gain.

These cognitive biases are strong because they are often interlinked and reinforcing. The danger is they impact decision-making processes, and may combine in a way to produce unexpected and not necessarily, positive outcomes.

I remember learning about the Bay of Pigs invasion when I was in high school. The invasion began when a CIA-financed and trained group of Cuban refugees landed in Cuba, with the objective of toppling Fidel Castro's communist-led government. The plan had been signed off by the then United States President, John F. Kennedy, and it was a disaster. Studies of this event have shown that there were numerous issues that gave rise to the decision-making failures including: deference to authority, different opinions being dismissed and groupthink. Interestingly, many of the President's advisers had doubts about the plan, but they suspended their judgment and didn't say anything because they thought everything he did was going to succeed. They were blinded by their opinion of him.

In business, sunk cost traps are another perfect example. They're evident in organisations all the time. The organisation has made a decision to invest in a project and they will keep throwing money at it despite the fact that logic and evidence may dictate that it's time to wrap it up. People don't like to admit they've made mistakes, and once an investment has been made it's often easier to keep going.

The project team and sponsor can easily convince themselves to ignore information that shows them it's time to do something different.

It takes great courage to admit that an investment you've made is wrong. It also takes great insight and personal awareness to admit that there is a better way. Having worked on large-scale projects in big corporates I've seen this play out many times. Sometimes the dollars at stake were large and yet often reputational matters were of greater concern than the costs. The executive group that signed off on the expenditure was concerned about what it would look like if they stopped the project and naturally the project team was worried about keeping their jobs. The players involved often let their biases unconsciously invade their decision-making.

Having awareness that bias pervades decision-making is important, but it is only helpful if you do something about it.

STEP TWO: Analyse your triggers and actions

There are always different perspectives on what is right and wrong – particularly on issues that are ambiguous or complex. This means that good people can do things that can be perceived as bad, unfair or unethical from another person's perspective. It is not a black and white world!

To remain centred you need to objectively analyse what is going on around you. This includes accepting yourself and embracing the doubt that comes with knowing you don't have all the answers – and that that's OK.

We can all build walls around ourselves. We do this to protect ourselves. And we can keep our eyes closed to possibilities and new beginnings. But, being in the dark and closed away from reality is not healthy. Having your eyes and heart open is crucial if you are to thrive in today's environment.

Being authentic, comfortable to show vulnerability and naturally curious are important qualities if you want to be centred. People who are uncomfortable with themselves and have low self-esteem are more easily persuaded by other people. We all have a desire for acceptance – to fit in and to be loved. When you feel unaccepted, you'll either try to conform or rebel. However, if you love yourself and who you are, you are less worried about what people think of you. This doesn't mean you don't want to be loved and respected, but you understand that not everyone you meet will like you, and that's OK. The most important person that needs to like you – is you!

Plus, if you know who you are, understand your trigger points and are happy with yourself, you are less likely to be enticed or led astray by others. This includes being led astray by the expectations imposed on you by others. Expectations can be helpful, but in many cases they can be a constraint that holds you back from being the best version of you.

To break away from expectations you need to know yourself and what you want out of life. It's impossible to stay centred when you don't know your core purpose. This isn't easy and we often struggle with what this means. People who know their purpose are more easily able to overcome obstacles and to forge their unique path. They have the confidence to take charge and be in control of crucial personal decisions, which ultimately determine the course of their life.

There have been some brilliant books written about the steps you can take to identify your purpose and help assess the congruence with your life. Bill George's *True North* is one example.[20] It is worth reading as it takes you through a series of exercises you can do to achieve better alignment in your personal and professional life.

People find their purpose in different ways. For some people uncovering their purpose is about study, experimentation or trying new things. For other people it's about helping others, taking risks or venturing into the unknown.

Cheryl Strayed who wrote about her journey from 'lost to found' in the novel *Wild* was one such person. She embarked on the three-month trek across the Pacific Crest Trail, covering more than 1,700 kilometres from Mexico to near the Canadian border. Relatively unprepared for the hike she discovered much about herself and her resilience and fortitude through the journey.

In a different arena, Kathryn Bigelow broke the mould for women film-makers. Movies such as 'Hurt Locker' and 'Zero Dark Thirty' were not the types of films that women in the industry made. She ignored that. She said: *"If there's specific resistance to women making movies, I just choose to ignore that as an obstacle for two reasons: I can't change my gender, and I refuse to stop making movies."*[21]

It's easy to be influenced by what is going on around you. If you don't like yourself and accept yourself, flaws and all, you're more open to the influence of others. This influence may not be good for you.

What's even more dangerous is that you can close your eyes to what is really happening around you because of your desire to fit in and be liked. That heightens the chance of you being unaware of the potentially dangerous impact the environment or culture is having on your ethical fibre.

The best option is to be constantly vigilant. This isn't easy and it's made harder by the fact that life is not clear-cut and there are always shades of grey, creating confusion and sometimes conflicted thoughts as to the best approach to take. Self-doubt can be a good thing because it means you are questioning what you are doing. You are being purposeful and thoughtful. Self-doubt is natural. Everyone has it in some form.

Self-doubt is a bad thing when it overwhelms you and stops you from progressing. Rather than see it as a negative, see it as a positive and recognise the service it can deliver to you. It is operating as a service to you and your need for progress.

Most people when they meet me for the first time think I'm incredibly confident. Deep down I'm not. In fact, most people have fears and insecurities. The difference is whether you let them define you and hold you back or propel you forward.

I've always lived my life by the motto: "Feel the fear and do it anyway". I'll often do things where I am incredibly nervous, but I know if I'm not nervous I'm not pushing myself hard enough. It was like that when I went for jobs. I made some, seemingly, fairly radical jumps in my career. One of my friends once said to me: "Michelle your career terrifies me". In a funny way, my career scared me too but I knew that if I didn't feel scared when I accepted a new role I was taking a too-safe option.

Embracing yourself and using doubt as leverage is a step in the right direction. So too is taking the time to understand your level of consciousness when you are making decisions.

To help remove bias you need to be highly aware of your present state and your thinking. This is meta-cognition. Thinking about how you think and process information is only useful if you take the time to examine the bias that can creep into it, and what situational factors may give rise to it.

This isn't easy. It takes immense courage to critically look into yourself to see what is going on for you. It is even harder to distinguish if there is a difference between what you are thinking and saying, and actually doing. That is, when there is a difference between your espoused theory and your theory in use.

Look for triggers and ask yourself, are you likely to have bias in this situation due to:

- Past experience
- Background and upbringing
- Opinions of friends or people you respect

- Cultural conditioning
- Uncertainty and a desire to fit in.

After you've done that, consider how you can expand your field of view to take on different opinions and perspectives.

☑ CHECKPOINT ACTIVITY

When you are making an important decision how often do you do the following:

- ☐ Seek information from people outside your normal circle of friends or colleagues
- ☐ Ensure you are not overwhelmed by too much information or detail at the one time
- ☐ Spend time prioritising the information and use a clear process to sort, rank and select the possible outcomes
- ☐ Critically consider what bias could be at play in the situation
- ☐ Try to remain curious and opened-minded throughout the decision-making process, and recognise that you don't know everything
- ☐ Consider if you are letting 'System 1' or 'System 2' drive the decision (refer page 64)
- ☐ Take the time to analyse the decision from multiple perspectives
- ☐ Sleep on the decision because looking at the issue the next morning will often provide you with a fresh perspective.

These are all building blocks that will help you build an aptitude for effective decision-making – where your integrity remains centred.

STEP THREE: Construct your aptitude

Aptitude is your willingness to challenge assumptions and pre-conceived ideas and to take on different ideas and opinions.

Constructing an effective aptitude takes energy and a willingness to put in place four primary practices:

- Learning from mistakes
- Picking your timing
- Practising self-care
- Using structure to help avoid bias.

It is not enough to just do one of these practices. If you're eager to build the habit of better decision-making, you will want to put all of them to good use.

Practice One: Make learning-filled mistakes

No one is perfect, and everyone makes mistake. Despite your best efforts, sometimes things will not go to plan. Not every decision you make will be right. That's OK. Learn from the decision and keep moving forward.

As Orlando A. Battista, a Canadian chemist and author said: *"An error doesn't become a mistake until you refuse to correct it".*

Being willing to step forward and admit mistakes can be hard but it is core to maintaining your integrity. If you are unwilling to see that you can and have made a mistake, you are lying to yourself and those around you. Eventually, it eats you up.

Khaled Hosseini's novel, *The Kite Runner*, spells this out in beautiful prose. The story which spans a number of decades, starts with two young boys from different sides of the racial divide in Afghanistan. A lie from one has a profound impact on the other boy's circumstances. But, it was the boy who lied who lived with the guilt and regret, which ultimately propelled him to make amends.

Many business leaders have failed and gone on to build very successful careers and businesses. It is not the mistake that defined them but what they did with the learning from that mistake. If you are to be centred you need to know when you have made a mistake, and realise who has been impacted by that mistake. Make amends for any negative impact. Be quick to apologise and seek restitution. And then examine what happened. Don't beat yourself up but be curious about it.

Ask yourself these questions:

- What happened?
- Why did it happen?
- Could I have prevented it from happening?
- How am I getting a good return on investment from the mistake – such that I am taking away rich learnings from every element of the mistake?
- What would I do differently next time?
- What would I not change?

Practice Two: Time decisions to your advantage

As we become more tired we become more reliant on our System 1 brain. There is simply not enough capacity in our pre-frontal cortex to cover all the decisions we make each day.

What the research shows is that as you become more skilled at a task, less energy is required to perform it. What this means in practice is that as you become more skilled at something, it becomes more familiar to the brain and so less cognitive effort is required to perform it.

Think back to when you were a child and learning how to tie your shoe laces. It wasn't easy. I remember my nana showing me how to do it 'bunny ear' style and my mum showing me a different way. Both ways felt clunky. I had to consciously think about every step in the process, and yet it was a very simple process. Of course, it didn't take long to hard-wire that process into my brain and soon the task was performed effortlessly.

Each time you do something new your brain is building a new neural pathway. The more frequently you do something, the deeper the neural pathway becomes and so it becomes easier to remember and do again in the future.

You need to treat the brain as a precious resource. This means you do the most intensive, energy depleting activities first thing in the morning. Don't waste energy on checking emails or social media. Instead, if you are writing a report, or trying to solve a complex problem do that first thing in the morning. Decisions that are complex and difficult are also best made when your brain is most alert – this is usually as early in the day as possible. You can then schedule the less mind-taxing things for later in the day.

Practice Three: Care for your heart, soul and body

Teachings from Eastern religions provide useful food for thought, regardless of religious beliefs. Putting to one side the specific religious elements, these teachings offer wonderful insights into humanity and what can be done to live a whole and just life.

In Zen philosophy they talk about the 'Four Limbs of Leadership'. These four limbs are: enlightenment and virtue, speech and action, humaneness and justice, etiquette and law. In teachings, the writer uses the metaphor of a tree. *"Enlightenment and virtue are the root of the teaching; humaneness and justice are the branches of the teaching. With no root, it is impossible to stand; with no branches it is impossible to be complete".* [22] What the writer is saying is we need to embrace our whole selves to lead a full life, and this requires balance.

This is about looking after our whole selves: our physiology, neurology and psychology. Think of it like the body (physiology), the brain (neurology) and the heart/emotions (psychology). This is not a scientifically correct way to think about it, as scientists tell us that all emotions start in the brain and are then translated into a physiological response in the body. However, it is useful to think about how we manage our whole selves – not just part of our selves – because all of these elements in the body are interrelated.

If you go back to the 'fight or flight' aspects I discussed in the section on mindset, it has particular relevance in the context of integrity and decision-making.

For example, if you feel threatened by a boss at work there will be a whole raft of instinctive acts that take place. But, most importantly, when your limbic system (which includes your amygdala) is aroused it decreases the resources that are available for your pre-frontal cortex. Remember, this is where the executive functions such as reasoning, analysis and problem-solving take place. When this happens you're more likely to make mistakes, have reduced working memory, be more pessimistic, and less likely to solve complex problems. To top it all off, you're also more likely to react defensively.

This means that when you face challenging situations you may not be best placed to make rational and well thought out decisions. It is in times such as these that you can veer off course. When you feel angry and frustrated you're less likely to consider the consequences of your actions and you're less able to see the other person's perspective.

This is where techniques such as mindfulness can once again play an important role. It's about calming yourself down so you can then calm the situation down, to make a rational and well-reasoned decision.

Similarly, staying fit and healthy also enables you to better regulate your emotions and to find ways to expel unused frustrations and anger which, if left unresolved, can be physically and emotionally harmful.

Practice Four: Use structure to keep out the bias

There are structural approaches you can adopt to help remove bias. For example, using checklists helps you ensure that all bases are covered. Having a clear assessment or decision-making criteria can assist you to ensure that decisions made are more impartial and reason-based.

You can also 'blind' information so that you are not coloured by your bias. For example, some companies remove names and dates of birth from resumes so the person reviewing the CV only assesses it based on skills and experiences, and is not influenced by gender, ethnicity or age.

Research has shown how successful this can be in improving the representation of women. For example, an orchestra which had the musicians play behind a screen during auditions saw the level of female representation in the orchestra increase from 5% to 40% over a number of years.[23]

Change is never linear and things will go off track, so being open to new ideas and information is critical if you want to be able to step up and influence. You don't want to be the last person to know what is really going on, and you don't want to be building a culture of denial.

Being open to all types of news – the good, the bad and the really bad is important. You do this when you:

- Welcome all types of news – even news that is difficult to hear. Not only is your reaction a test of your character, it sets the standard for what happens in the future. If you shoot the messenger, next time an issue arises, you're less likely to find people willing to alert you to it.

- Talk to people at all levels of the organisation. Hierarchy can interfere with the information you receive as information can be filtered and sanitised before it hits your desk. People don't want to look bad and they want to paint the most optimistic picture of what is happening. Talking with people across, and up and down the organisational hierarchy ensures you have a better handle on what is happening.

- Beware of gatekeepers, particularly if you are in a leadership role. While your support staff will often be acting with good intent, if access to you is so heavily managed that it is impossible for people to see you, you will find it harder to have a realistic assessment of progress and issues.
- Take the time to walk the floor. Casually walking around the office and stopping to have incidental conversations is often an invaluable way of finding out what is going on. It's also a great way to build rapport and relationships with people.
- Invite differences of opinion. When you are making decisions make sure you have people with different perspectives and backgrounds involved. This will help you engage in a broad level of analysis and debate before deciding. Out-of-the-box thinking often comes from unexpected quarters.
- Be open to learning. News that something has gone wrong on a project or piece of work won't make you happy, but be open to the learning that it offers. It is better to fail fast than fail slow. Acknowledge the mistake, understand what caused it, and act swiftly to address it.
- Constantly be alert to the weak signals. This means you have your eyes wide open to what is going on around you, and are naturally curious and questioning. If something doesn't feel right, it usually isn't. Trust your gut instinct and keep asking questions until you get to the heart of the matter.
- Don't silence the dissenters. It is often the person with the dissenting opinion, or the person who is asking the probing questions, who will help you see the issue from a different perspective. While this can be frustrating, it is usually

helpful in the long run as you can take comfort from the fact that you have examined the issue from multiple angles.

- Be conscious that undiscovered issues are worse than discovered issues. Once a problem has been identified you can do something about it. However, when it's unknown and remains undetected for a long time, it's likely to cause even greater damage. Be grateful that the issue has been found, and you now have the opportunity to do something to fix it.

As you strive to unplug your bias and make good decisions it's worth remembering the quote from Alfred Sloan, the former CEO of General Motors. He understood the power of different opinions when making decisions. He said:

"Gentlemen, I take it we are all in complete agreement on the decision here…Then I propose we postpone further discussion on this matter until our next meeting to give ourselves time to develop disagreement and perhaps gain some understanding of what the decision is all about". [24]

4. Be always agile

> "Action is the foundational key to all success."
>
> —Pablo Picasso, Artist

People think of the term agile in many different ways. For some it's a methodology used in the IT software development industry or project implementations. For others it's about flexibility and adaptability, and using feedback loops to shape future actions. I like to use the term 'agile productivity', because for me being agile is absolutely connected with the goal of being productive. That is, getting things done well, and in the most efficient way possible.

If agile is the 'how you do it', the productivity is the effectiveness and efficiency of the 'outcome of how you do it'. To be an effective leader today you need to make the most of your time and be as productive as possible. There are many opportunities to get distracted and ways to waste time. At the same time, the expectations on people in organisations is significant – particularly if you're in a leadership role. If you want to succeed you have to know how to be agile and how to make progress.

I worked with a person who was incredibly smart, but he couldn't make a decision. It drove those around him, like me, nuts. He'd sit on decisions, prevaricate, make a decision and then change his mind. It felt like we were just going around in a circle and in a constant state of flux. The team felt constrained and held back, and we were working very long hours and getting nowhere. It had a huge impact on the team's morale.

From my perspective, it seemed as if he didn't trust me (and those around him) because he wouldn't let me (or others) make decisions. It was a real dilemma because he clearly didn't like making decisions but wouldn't delegate decision-making to other people. In the end, this inability to make decisions held him back from being as successful as he could have been.

If you want to be influential you have to be capable and comfortable with making decisions. You need to grasp the three core ingredients of agile productivity – being decisive, disciplined and determined. Successful people display these characteristics, and so they know how to make progress and stay ahead of the game. They use these qualities in both their personal and professional lives to best respond to their environment, new requirements and feedback.

When you are decisive you are also being deliberate. You are deliberate about what type of decision you are making and therefore what type of decision process you need to use. Is it a quick decision, such as 'will I have tea or coffee in the morning?' In which case, not a lot of analysis is required.

Or is it a complex, multi-faceted issue, which necessitates listening to other people's opinions, gathering facts and data, and whatever else you need to make a good decision?

For complex decisions, this process of gathering, sorting and reflecting is critical. Otherwise you are prone to making a reactionary or ill-considered decision. That is, to let your System 1 brain be in the driver's seat for the decision-making.

Being productive is also about having the right amount of discipline so you can move forward. Discipline is not a constraint. It's a motivator. You can define discipline negatively, but to do that is to miss its power. Discipline is about focus, and all successful people know how to leverage it.

M. Scott Peck, the author of the well-known self-help book *The Road Less Traveled* said: "Without discipline we can solve nothing. With only some discipline we can solve only some problems. With total discipline we can solve all problems".[25]

The combination of decisiveness and discipline is powerful. It is at this intersection that you start to make intentional progress. This is progress that is purposeful, planned and well executed. If you take action but have no idea where you are going and have no clear plan to get you there, you aren't being disciplined. Instead you are wasting your time – and probably the time of the people around you.

This is like getting in a car and having no destination or idea of how to navigate to your destination. You'll just end up spending a lot of time and resources wandering around.

This is why strategy and planning are so critical. People often think about strategic planning and execution only in an organisational context, and yet they are incredibly helpful processes for your everyday life. This is career and life planning in action. Having a goal or guiding direction on where you want to get to, and what you need to do to get there, is really useful. It helps to focus your activities, mind and energy. It also helps you develop the skills and ideas that build your agility and responsiveness – enabling you to grasp unanticipated opportunities and be productively agile.

Once you start executing the plan it can feel like one step forward, two steps backwards. This is why you need to be able to overcome setbacks and be determined to achieve the desired outcome. By being determined you are willing to try new things and persist when things don't work out. You'll also be smart enough to know when something isn't working and you should therefore stop, adapt and try something different.

If you want to maintain momentum, you need the balance of determination and discipline.

Larry Bossidy and Ram Charan in their book *Execution: The discipline of getting things* done repeat the well-known saying: *"We don't think ourselves into a new way of acting, we act ourselves into a new way of thinking"*.[26]

People who are successful take action. They know how to learn from their mistakes, overcome setbacks and keep moving forward. Importantly, they also know how to leverage opportunities. They can see the opportunities to be seized. They act decisively and if one opportunity fails, they look for another. They know how to find opportunities and to make the most of them (see Figure 12).

Figure 12: The Agile Productivity Model

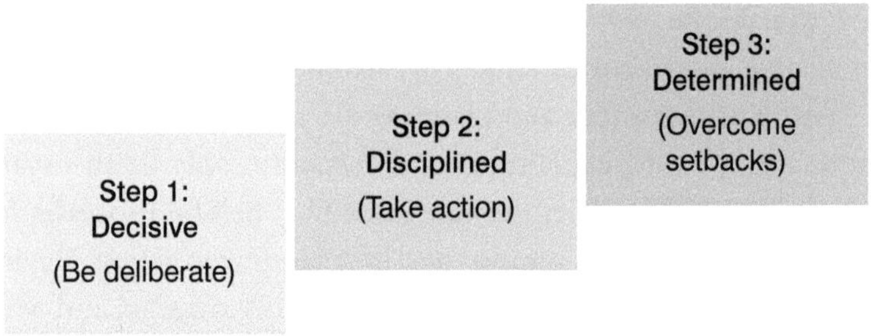

Step 1: Decisive (Be deliberate)

Step 2: Disciplined (Take action)

Step 3: Determined (Overcome setbacks)

MASTER THE GAME OF PROGRESS

> "If you don't know where you're going, any road will take you there."
> —The Cheshire Cat from "Alice in Wonderland"

To master the game of progress and make sustained momentum you will want to successfully craft the skills of decisiveness, discipline and determination. But what steps do you take so they're ingrained in your personal and professional life?

I liken it to going on a trek through the mountains. To safely arrive at your destination you need to make decisions, be disciplined in the approach you take and be determined to finish. To do this you make decisions before you leave: you plan the trek and the route that you are going to take. This helps to guide you forward so you know the level of difficulty and the challenges you may encounter. You use discipline to prepare yourself – mentally and physically – for the trek, which includes being clear on your goals and why you want to complete the trek, and ensuring your physical preparedness for it. This training gives you a clear idea of what you need to do throughout the journey and helps to safeguard you should things go wrong. It puts you in the best physical and mental state to be able to make decisions. This mental preparedness also helps your determination. At the same time, having a really clear purpose for the trek gives you the best chance of finishing it, even if there are setbacks. It is this combination that helps to ensure success.

STEP ONE: Be decisive

Being decisive is about understanding your decision-making framework and backing yourself to make decisions. Have you ever thought about how you make a decision? Is the process random or planned? Does it matter?

If you recall the section on our 'automatic brain', our brain uses energy-saving devices in decision-making. To conserve energy it takes short-cuts, quickly discarding what it sees as extraneous pieces of information in the decision-making process. This is a very helpful skill. The brain's ability to process hundreds of pieces of information simultaneously is really important. This subconscious processing and making of decisions means we can get stuff done relatively effortlessly. We don't have to consciously make a decision every time we need to breathe, yawn or sleep. Additionally, as less familiar tasks become more familiar we use less of the brain's decision-making power.

Think about the first time you sat behind the wheel of a car. Everything felt strange, and as the process of driving was explained your brain was rapidly processing the information. It felt unnatural and required an enormous amount of concentration. There were lots of things to think about at the same time and the process didn't feel simple: turn the engine on; check mirrors; put the car into drive; press the accelerator and so on. At every step you had to think about what you were doing. Over time, it became automatic as the process of driving moved from your short-term to long-term memory. Now you may sometimes feel like you are driving without thinking about what you are doing.

What do you do when the decision is new or complex? What benefits are there in using a planned process?

> **STEP UP TIP**
>
> Never avoid making a decision. No decision is a decision in itself. I've worked in organisations where senior leaders avoided making decisions. For them, not making a decision was safer than making a decision. This was incredibly frustrating for the people who worked with them.

On the whole, people working in organisations want to get stuff done. They want to see progress. A lack of progress is one of the biggest de-motivators. Additionally, failing to make small decisions can lead to bigger issues down the track. It's often the culmination of the failure of many small decisions that leads to larger more disastrous outcomes.

I'm often reminded of the old proverb:

For want of a nail, the shoe was lost
For want of a shoe, the horse was lost
For want of a horse, the rider was lost
For want of a rider, the battle was lost
For want of a battle, the kingdom was lost.

If you don't like making decisions you need to find a way to get comfortable with it. For people who struggle to make a decision, having a process to follow can be useful. The decision-making process doesn't need to be burdensome and it should vary according to the size, nature and complexity of the decision that is being made. There are some decisions that can be made quickly and instinctually, and some that need to be slower and more deliberate.

An instinctual decision may be what you want to wear in the morning or what type of tea to drink. These are everyday life decisions that don't need to consume a lot of mental energy. I once heard the story that apparently Barack Obama owns only two different styles of suits – so that he doesn't waste mental energy deciding what to wear.

For more complex decisions that require some thought it is useful to think of the process you can use and the steps you can take.

A simple process can look like this:

- **Clarify the problem** – One of the most important steps is to be really clear on the problem you are trying to solve. It's easy to assume that your interpretation of the problem is the same as your colleague's interpretation. This may not be the case. Spending time being clear on the problem is a good investment of time.

- **Listen for ideas** – Gather information on the problem by talking to people, listening to their ideas and researching the problem. As you do this, don't discard information too quickly. This means you need to suspend judgment, and take on information from a broad range of sources. Be particularly open to listening to different opinions, and to people who hold contrary views to yours. Sometimes the best ideas come from left field, or from ideas that initially make you feel uncomfortable. Take the time to orient and explore the idea.

- **Reflect on options** – Sort, synthesise and analyse the information. Take the time to understand the options (benefits and drawbacks). Look at the ideas from multiple perspectives. Be conscious of the impact of the options, and rank the impacts and benefits. Ask yourself: what do I want to discard or add to this idea? Sometimes ideas are made better by tweaking around the edges – not all of the idea will necessarily be bad or good. The best way forward is often a blend of ideas and concepts. Depending on the complexity of the problem or decision you may do this step multiple times.

- **Decide the approach** – Develop decision-making criteria and use these to assess the best course of action. From there you can easily make a conscious decision, fully aware of the facts and consequences (both positive and negative) of the decision. This may involve testing and evaluating a few of the options before selecting the path to take.

Remember, decision-making is not always a linear process and sometimes the solution is not easy to find. Feeling comfortable making a decision in a complex and ambiguous environment where you have incomplete data is challenging. It helps if you can accept that making progress involves learning from your mistakes. As the saying goes: fail fast, fail often, and fail meaningfully. If you're never failing, then I'd suggest you're not pushing yourself hard enough and you're certainly not taking yourself outside your comfort zone.

Scientists spend a lot of time failing. Each failure is a sign of progress, as they know they can now discount that element in their hypothesis. They don't just look for evidence to support their hypothesis. They actively look for evidence to disprove it. They keep applying different types of thinking and processes to help uncover the solution. They explore, examine, alter their approach, test the idea and then iterate until the desired outcome is realised or scientific puzzle is solved. Scientific breakthroughs are based on many, many failures.

As part of this decision-making process you can and should listen to your instincts. Instincts are real feelings that should not be dismissed. Get to know your instincts and to trust your gut instincts, because your gut is a powerful decision-aiding tool. To highly analytical people this can sound counter-intuitive. There is no doubt that for decisions that have personal consequences your body will let you know how you are feeling about that decision. This isn't about ignoring assumptions and blind spots, which can lead to bad decisions. Instead it is being conscious of how a decision makes you feel.

I always remember the time when I was making the decision to stay in corporate life or do something else. I had worked in the corporate sphere for more than 20 years, and was in the top 5% of wage-earners so it would have been easy to stay. I was called by two large companies about particular roles and I didn't feel excited or happy. I remember at the time thinking: *Wow – this is my body telling me something. It's time to get out and do something different.* Listening to my body in that situation was important and I made the decision to set up my own company. While people saw that decision as courageous, for me it wasn't because it just felt like the right thing to do.

Once you understand the process to use for making decisions, it's time to embrace your capacity to make decisions. Making decisions is good for the soul because it helps you have control. Think of it like this.

Making decisions is often about change. Many people think they can't control change, and therefore they let change overwhelm them. While the decision to make a change that impacts you may not be under your control (for example, because it has been made by senior management), how you react and plan for the change is within your control. There's nothing wrong with expressing sadness or disappointment with respect to a change. These are healthy, natural emotions. However, it's important to find a way to help steer your emotions towards positivity and optimism. One way to do this is to start taking control by making decisions on those things that you can control.

The word 'control' often has negative connotations, but in the case of change it can be liberating. People usually find change stressful because they feel they are not in control of what is happening to them. To feel in control you need to take control. You do this by: steering your own course, working through what the change means for you and determining what you want to do about it.

As part of this process, understand what decisions you can and can't make. As well, map out a range of different approaches, noting the benefits and drawbacks of each of these options, and then make a decision as to what course you will take. This is the clarify, listen, reflect and decide approach I outlined earlier.

Feeling like you have a choice in your response to change gives you fortitude. When you find you have options you will feel more in control. Having a sense of control is really important. Research has shown that feeling like you have no control over your life has serious consequences for your health.

Dan Gardner recounts the story of nursing home residents. When they had all their control taken away (in this case, their ability to make any decisions) the number of residents who died in a year increased from 15% to 30%.[27]

In the context of organisational change think about how you can become 'active' with the change, and get involved. Be the person who volunteers to be part of the change initiative's change network, or the person who volunteers to be involved in the pilot program. That way, you will be ahead of the curve and you'll have first-hand knowledge of the change and what it could mean. You'll also get the opportunity to try new things and new ways of behaving.

STEP TWO: Be disciplined

The Latin phrase – *Otia dant vitia* – means idleness begets vice. While the phrase still holds true, in a modern context, we have the opposite problem. We live in a world with lots of noise, information and things that are vying for our attention. It's very easy to get distracted.

Have you ever counted how many times a day you check your emails or social media? When you're alerted to a new email, SMS or social media item do you quickly switch your focus from your current task to that alert?

We all love to believe that we're brilliant multi-taskers. However, the sad reality is we aren't. When you multi-task your attention is fractioned, and as you switch from one activity to another you lose concentration and ultimately become less productive. If you are sitting in a meeting and typing an email you won't be fully concentrating on what is being said in the meeting. You may think you're listening but you won't hear the entire conversation or fully interpret the information being delivered. This is particularly because much of what is communicated is transmitted non-verbally.

At the same time, each time you switch from one task to another your brain is activated and that uses up precious resources. Our brains just aren't hard-wired to handle multiple issues simultaneously or to rapidly switch back and forth between tasks.

David Rock, in his brilliant book *Your Brain at Work* uses the metaphor of the pre-frontal cortex as a stage. Issues arise when there are too many actors on your stage, each trying to play multiple scenes. He notes, *"While it is physically possible sometimes to do several mental tasks at once, accuracy and performance drop off quickly"*.[28]

This is backed up by research which shows that momentary shifts from one task to another, such as stopping to respond to an SMS, increases the amount of time necessary to finish the primary task by as much as 25%.[29] It is far better to work in 60 to 90 minute bursts, where you are focused on one task.

Multi-tasking almost feels like a necessity because there is an incredible sense of busyness in today's work environment. There always seems to be so much to do. When you're asked "How are you?" does the word busy figure in the answer? For many people the answer would be "Yes". When you combine this busyness with the need to get lots done and the ineffective use of multi-tasking, there's a real danger that you achieve little because your attention is fragmented and unfocused. You keep pedalling hard, but you're not getting very far.

To make progress and enable higher-quality, more productive work, think about how you can be disciplined and not fracture your attention. I think of it as the 'Three A's of Discipline': attitude, attention and action.

1. **Attitude** – Attitude is a state of mind that means you are conscious of precisely what you need to get the job done effectively and efficiently. It's about being prepared to listen

and reflect, and being present with the task at hand. This targeted concentration enables you to ignore the distractions and extraneous activities that divert you from making progress. With the right attitude you are really clear on how you approach the task so that you are doing it in the most effective way possible.

Challenge yourself. If you think something will take four months, ask yourself what you need to do to deliver it in half the time. Don't let yourself get caught up in unnecessary bureaucracy. For example, don't email someone – talk to them. Email can be a real trap because it can lock you into a messy and needlessly time wasting conversation. Often it takes longer to write the email than it does to speak with someone. So don't avoid talking to people – particularly as talking is essential for building constructive relationships.

2. **Attention** – When you pay attention you are focused on the task in front of you and giving yourself enough time and space to devote to it. To do this you need to know the steps to take every day to reach your goals. This takes a little planning – not too much – you don't want to over-plan as that's a waste of time too.

   It's also helpful to consider doing work in dedicated chunks of time. Highly productive people will tell you that they time-box their work day, and set aside the morning for highly complex thinking. They also ruthlessly manage their schedule to ensure they don't waste time. They know how to use their brain energy purposefully.

3. **Action** – Lastly, when you apply action you are clear on the purpose of the task and have the skills, plans and

patience to carry them through. You know how to pay attention to and prioritise your actions.

When you are clear on what you need to achieve each day to secure your desired goals it becomes easier to know what you can say 'no' to. Saying 'no' helps you stay focused on what is really important. It's also about being clear on why you want to do this because if the motivation is missing it will be hard to follow through and maintain your determination.

I've found these three elements to be really helpful. Particularly when I feel overwhelmed by the amount of work I need to get done in a set timeframe. I find by focusing, planning and breaking the tasks down into bite-size pieces it doesn't feel so challenging. It becomes about what I need to do each day to keep moving forward.

STEP THREE: Be determined

The scouts have a motto – 'Be prepared'. It's a good motto to embrace when you are working in an organisation because invariably something will go off track. It is comforting to know that the world's most successful people have often faced adversity and challenges, and they've experienced failure. What is different is that they haven't let those events hold them back. They try, persist and adapt.

Interestingly, successful people are often not the most gifted in their chosen field. We are led to believe that it's innate talent that drives success, whereas it's actually determination. If you Google the words "successful people who were told they had no talent" you'll find names such as: Jackson Pollock, Marcel Proust, Elvis Presley, Ray Charles, Lucille Ball and Charles Darwin.

There are also countless examples of very successful business people who struggled at school and then went on to be spectacularly successful in business, or people whose original ideas or concepts were initially rejected. Jackson Pollock, one of the world's most famous artists, was never considered naturally gifted as a painter. Instead, he focused on how he could hone his craft – and get better and better at it. It was this drive and determination that led to his success.

It is important to recall the earlier section in this book on mindsets at this juncture. Your mindset will play a huge part in the extent to which you are resilient and don't let setbacks hold you back. Having an empowered mindset where you embrace learning and see the opportunities for growth is essential.

What successful people have in common is they understand that the failure they have experienced doesn't define them. What defines them is what they do with that failure. They see it as a learning opportunity.

Determination is critical when you are working in a world undergoing constant change. Making progress can feel like a series of ups and downs. Some days it feels easy. Other days it feels hard. And that's because progress isn't a linear process.

To maintain your resilience and determination it's important to manage your energy levels as you try, persist and adapt your actions to keep making progress. Managing your energy levels helps you stay focused and in the best physical and mental shape. Once again, knowing what to say no to, and having the courage to do that is critical. Don't waste your precious energy on things that don't matter, or things that won't help you reach your goal.

Determination and discipline go hand in hand. It is much easier to maintain your determination when you are really clear on your purpose. I've always believed that if you put your mind to something you can do it. If you want to learn to ski – you can do it. If you want to lose 5 kilograms – you can do it.

But, it's much easier to do this if the reason for wanting to do it is crystal clear. Of course, that purpose needs to be relevant for you – not someone else. What do I mean by that? When you are making a personal change, the reason for the change needs to hold relevance and resonance for you. If you are making the change for someone else, it is much easier not to change.

When your purpose is clear, setbacks – while disappointing – don't hold you back. They become amazing opportunities for learning and reflection. With anything you do in life that really matters there will be challenges. How you approach those challenges will impact your ability to overcome them. You will become very quickly drained of energy if you let the challenges overwhelm you. Finding ways to break the challenges down into smaller pieces, being clear on the progress you are making and celebrating that progress all help in this regard.

Rosabeth Moss Kanter talks about how *"everything can look like a failure in the middle"*.[30] How true that is.

✓ CHECKPOINT ACTIVITY

To make progress through the 'hard middles' consider how you can apply the following suggestions:

- ☐ Draw on your resilience. Make sure you are taking time to take care of yourself and those around you. It is at times such as this that stress levels can feel unmanageable – causing significant health issues. Be wary of this and alert to the danger signs for you and your team.

- ☐ Don't lose focus. Your strength of character is being tested. Team members and colleagues will be looking to you for guidance and direction. Be available, supportive and encouraging to those around you, and find ways to keep moving forward.

- ☐ Seek guidance and advice from those around you. There will be lots of people who will have ideas about what you should do. Know who you need to listen to, and be open to the voices of dissent as they can provide useful perspectives too. Also, be conscious that you don't need to have all the answers. The wisdom usually comes from the group – so seek it out.

- ☐ Make decisions effectively and swiftly. In times of challenge, people can become reluctant to make decisions. However, it is at precisely this time that the need to make decisions is greatest. People are looking for leadership and making a decision goes with the territory.
- ☐ Look on this as a learning opportunity. Out of every failure or mistake there are immense opportunities to learn. It is only when you learn that you grow. So while you may not enjoy the experience, you will certainly benefit from it.

When things start to go pear-shaped, be thankful that you have the mindset and fortitude to learn through it. Most importantly, as you step up and build your influence continue to try, persist and adapt your approach and actions.

STAY AHEAD OF THE GAME

> "The difference between a beginner and the master is that the master practices a whole lot more."
>
> —*Yehudi Menuhin, Famous Violinist*

To stay ahead of the game you need to back yourself. Like time, your life is made up of the past, present and future. Are you looking to the past, the future or the present? Reflecting on the past helps with learning. Thinking about your future helps with goal-setting. Being present and using your time wisely helps advance you towards those goals.

Reflecting on the past, thinking about your future goals, and being focused on what you need to do in the present is a delicate balance. You need to look behind you – but not for so long that you get fixated on the past. You need to focus on the present – but not to the extent that you are so focused on present enjoyment that you don't plan for the future. Looking ahead means you scan the horizon. When you do this you can take a step back and see the bigger picture. This perspective is important as it helps you understand what may be changing in a world and societal context, and what you need to do to stay ahead of the game.

Being willing to learn, grow and adapt is critical. This love of learning in your personal life and career will help set you apart from others. You may know the ancient Chinese proverb:

If you want to plan for a day – plant rice
If you want to plan for a year – plant a tree
If you want to plan for a lifetime – educate.

Education is fundamental. If you want a healthy mind you need to be consciously aware of why you need to feed it, how you feed it, and what you feed it.

This involves applying a future-focused mindset to the concepts of being decisive, deliberate and determined. This helps you stay ahead of the game.

STEP ONE: Embrace learning to change

It's stating the obvious to say we live in changing times, because we do, and we always have. Everyone experiences change. However, the nature of the change varies substantially. Its source can be individually or externally driven (i.e. from environment, society, or politics) or it can be organisational. Its level of impact can range from being minor to transformational. Its pace can be steady or rapid. The only point of similarity is that change is constant.

It's time to fall in love with change and to embrace the skills needed to thrive through it. If you need convincing here are ten reasons why it's time to love change and the learning that accompanies it:

1. The pace of change isn't getting any slower and it's not going away. There's no point resisting it, so you might as well embrace it.
2. Change doesn't need to be 'change for change's sake', but it is only through change that the world, your organisation, your community, etc., can become better places.
3. It would be very boring if nothing ever changed and never changing runs counter to how humans have evolved.
4. Seeing change as an opportunity, rather than a threat, helps to change your mindset so that you are ready for the experience.
5. Everyone feels some form of discomfort during a change. That's normal and it's nothing to be afraid of. Accept the uncertainty.
6. Change is about learning and doing new things, and research shows that learning and growth is really good for your health – mind, body and soul.
7. If you are not prepared to learn, reflect and evolve you will fall behind everyone else which can negatively impact your career, lifestyle and happiness.
8. The more you understand yourself and how you react during periods of change, the more you are able to support yourself through change.
9. Think of change like an experiment – you never quite know what you are capable of doing and you may be delighted with the results.
10. The world is an amazing place – open yourself up to the opportunities that lie ahead.

Are you convinced yet? Being able to prosper through change is a fundamental life skill.

There's no doubt that some people find change harder than others. People are born with certain traits which are then styled and conditioned by their experiences and environment. The combination of these factors means that some people are more predisposed than others to cope with change well. Despite that fact, there are steps that everyone can take to increase their resilience and ability to cope with change. Mastering them provides not only useful life skills but skills that will help you become more effective and influential at work.

The first step is to embrace a love of learning. To thrive through changing environments you need to adapt, and to adapt you need to be willing to learn new things.

Children learn all the time, and often through playing. If you watch them, they are continually experimenting and when they fail at something, chances are they quickly dust themselves off and try again. This doesn't mean there aren't tears or tantrums, but children typically keep getting back up and trying again.

This gets harder as you get older. You get more set in your ways, and you can become more reluctant to try new things and do things differently. Your inner voice, which can be quite loud, can hold you back as it voices a fear of failure, of being judged or being held up to ridicule. This voice needs to be ignored. To grow you need to take yourself outside your comfort zone – this is healthy! Each time you learn something new, or try something new, you are challenging your brain.

The brain is like a muscle – so it's just like taking your body to the gym! It's good for you. Exercising your brain releases natural growth factors and influences the neurotransmitters in your brain, which enhances its performance. Neurotransmitters communicate information from your brain to other parts of your body. For example, they tell your heart to beat and your lungs to inhale and exhale.

As you learn new things old neural pathways are altered and new ones are created. This means you can effectively re-wire your brain. How brilliant is that! The science of neuroplasticity has proven that the brain isn't 'hard' and immalleable but more like plastic. You can shape and mould your brain based on what you do and don't do. Your brain can grow and develop throughout your life.

If you never change and never try new things you are preventing your brain from developing. Embracing change and the opportunity it brings is a step forward in the right direction. Rather than see changing times as hard, it's time to change your mindset and focus on why you should love change.

STEP TWO: Learn with passion and reason

There are many myths that exist about how we learn. In recent times, many of the old learning styles have been dismissed as irrelevant. Do you remember being told that you were either an auditory, visual or kinesthetic learner? Or that you were a right or a left brain thinker? Turns out this is mostly rubbish. There are preferences to how people learn but all elements are used, so too both sides of your brain. There's no doubt that your brain influences how you learn.

> **STEP UP TIP**
> If you want to know more about this, read Harvard Professor, Howard Gardner's theory of multiple intelligences. It recognises that there are multiple types of intelligence, and people use and combine them in different ways to solve problems and get things done.

You need the right mix of passion and reason to build your capacity to learn and to remember. That is, to move information from short-term memory to long-term memory. To be most effective this needs to be a conscious process involving: focus, connections, time, practice and sleep.

If you want to learn and remember things you need to focus. And you need to focus on one thing at a time. Switching attention between things distracts you and makes learning more difficult. It makes it harder for your brain to remember, as it is constantly being asked to do multiple things. The brain works best when it is focused.

Your brain also works better when it is focusing for sustained periods of time for say 60 to 90 minutes, with a short break. Your brain, like any muscle, needs to take breaks.

I plan my day in 30 minute blocks. I know what I want to achieve in each of those 30 minutes, and I challenge myself to do it faster. I then reward myself with a break and get up from my desk and away from the computer for a few moments. This helps to refresh my brain and I also feel a sense of achievement when I see the progress I've made.

Your brain is a pattern-recognition machine and so it remembers best when you create connections and insights as you are learning. This can involve looking for ways to make the learning relevant for you. Remember, your brain and its massive filing system needs time to process and it needs to be done consciously. If you want to remember something, study the item, and then practise retrieving what you've learned. It is this retrieval process that takes information from short-term memory and moves it to long-term memory.

It also remembers best when there is an emotional connection with the information or event. If you think back in your life, the events that are easiest to remember had some form of emotion in them.

You also need to have the time to learn. Your memory grows over time, as you reflect and think about what you have learned. This thinking about what you have learned is important. It enables you to create the space for making sense and meaning out of what is happening. It is through sense-making that you generate insights, which are one of the most potent forms of learning. This will only happen if you space out your learning over time.

Trying to cram too much into your brain at any one time doesn't work. Think back to your days as a student when you were cramming for exams. You may have got through the exam – thanks to your short-term memory – but you are unlikely to have remembered much a couple of weeks after the exam.

Research has demonstrated that it is practice that makes mastery, not skill alone. Research from a team of psychologists in Germany in the 1990s showed that deliberate practice – not talent alone – was a factor in becoming an elite performer.[31] They looked at the practice habits of violin students from childhood through to adulthood. What they found was that while the students all started studying at the same time – age 5 – by the time they were 20, the elite performers had averaged more than 10,000 hours of practice, while the less able performers had only 4,000 hours of practice.

This is not to say that practice alone will make you successful, but what it does reveal is that practice and learning are crucial elements in determining your success.

You can use visualisation exercises to hone your skills. Research has shown that visualising doing something activates the same sections in the brain as if you were actually doing it. This is because your subconscious mind cannot distinguish the difference between doing something and visualising doing it. Sounds incredible, but it's true.

You can thank the mirror neurons in your brain for this remarkable feat. Your mirror neurons fire up when you act, as well as when you observe and act. This means you can gain skills through observation – not just direct experience. Consequently, using visualisation is a neat and valid way to learn and enhance your skills.

Elite athletes practise this all the time. They build a successful routine and visualise themselves in the competition and winning the race. If they're a runner they focus on the race. They visualise the start, the sound of the gun firing, and them running down the lane and finishing the race ahead of their competition. US Olympian, Michael Phelps, who won 22 swimming medals over three Olympiads, is known to have used this practice to great effect.

Once again, it takes practice. It's not a one-off event but something you do every day for a sustained period of time. You start by thinking about something you want to be good at. You then visualise yourself in that specific moment doing every step of the process very effectively. And you keep visualising this process over and over and over again.

Another key factor is sleep. When you sleep your memory is strengthened, and so getting an adequate amount of sleep each night is an important part of this process. A lack of sleep has the same impact on your brain as too much alcohol consumption. I find, particularly as I get older, that not getting enough sleep means I wake up the next morning feeling as if I am hung over. I know I need eight hours a night to function effectively. I may not always get eight hours but it's what I strive to achieve. Getting into a routine of going to bed and getting up at the same time each day is also important. It helps to regulate your sleep cycle.

☑ CHECKPOINT ACTIVITY

If you want to learn with passion and reason, and strengthen your ability to learn and remember, consider:

- How motivated are you to learn?

- What is the context of the learning and are you able to connect with it and make meaning of it?
- How much attention are you paying when you are processing the information, and are you distracted by other things around you?
- How tired are you, and are you sleep-deprived?

STEP THREE: Dominate your cravings

The saying goes: garbage in–garbage out. The same goes for your brain. If you never do anything to stretch your mind, your brain won't grow and develop. Think of it like a diet for your brain.

What's your diet and what's your appetite? What are you craving? Is your learning filled with whole, healthy learnings such as books, new learnings, ideas, etc., or is it the junk food diet with a constant stream of mindless television and YouTube clips? This is not to say that you can't learn anything from watching TV or YouTube clips but much of it is mindless. While television is a way of winding down, if that's all you consume it's incredibly unhealthy.

Do you crave learning? Are you ravenous for more – always curious about the world as there is so much more to learn? Or do you happily starve yourself – thinking there is nothing more to learn?

In short, is your learning stalled, slow, stunted or sustained?

If you want sustained 'brain' growth it's important to have the right balance of feeding your mind whole foods and having a healthy appetite for trying and learning new things (see Figure 13).

To stay ahead of the game, don't sit back and wait for someone to tell you what you need to learn – be proactive about it. Build your personal learning plan.

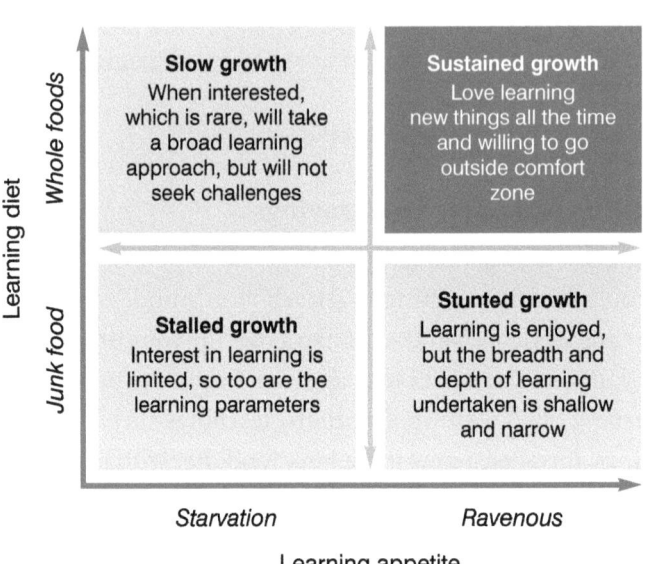

Figure 13: Balancing your learning diet and appetite for sustained brain growth

✓ CHECKPOINT ACTIVITY

Here are some suggestions for you to try:

☐ Buy a book on a topic that you have always wanted to know about, and that is not related to your day job. Read the book and soak in the learnings.

☐ If you sit in an office all day, attend a course that requires you to use your hands to create something (e.g. woodwork, craft or design).

☐ Go to a lecture on a subject that will broaden your field of vision.

☐ Subscribe to online news so you can receive up-to-date information and knowledge from around the world.

☐ Enrol in one of the free or low-cost courses or MOOC (mass open online courses) that are offered through sites like EdX, Coursera and Udemy. These courses are run by some of the world's most prestigious universities – and many of them are free. Want to go to Harvard, Stanford or Berkeley? You can. Just get online.

- [ ] Exercise regularly because the endorphins that are released through exercise stimulate connections in the brain.
- [ ] Undertake new experiences as they physically rewire the brain. They also make you a much more interesting person to be around, which is fantastic for when you make new connections and build relationships.
- [ ] Spend time outdoors and connect with nature. Smell the flowers. Listen to the sounds around you. Take your shoes off and walk in the grass. Feel the sensation. This is food for your soul.
- [ ] Travel and go to new destinations. Travel not only broadens the mind but it takes you outside your comfort zone – getting you to experience things in different ways.
- [ ] Get the right amount of sleep as loss of it hurts attention, executive function, working memory, mood, quantitative skills, logical reasoning and motor dexterity.
- [ ] Continue to meet and interact with new people. This is important not only from a networking perspective but because it helps you maintain strong levels of social engagement and connection.
- [ ] Stay relevant in your profession. It's important to continuously undertake personal development. If you want to be at the top of your game – you need to be abreast of the latest thinking and ideas from your profession, and also from complementary professions.

These activities are not supposed to be a chore. They should be fun. Think of it as a brilliant excuse to explore and experiment with new things and ideas, while helping you stay ahead of the game.

Part 2
The Organisation

5. Activate the system

> "The harder you push, the harder the system pushes back."
>
> —Peter Senge, Systems Scientist

Systems are complex, multi-faceted, interconnected and inter-related. They are made up of many players and many roles. However, these connections and intersections can be hard to find. Impacts can easily be overlooked and so it becomes hard to achieve progress. All of us are players in many different systems: organisational, family, social and community.

The concept of an organisation as a system has been around for a long time. Indeed, many of you will have used the metaphor of an organisation as an environmental ecosystem. Systems are on display in the environment all the time.

For example, plankton which are microscopic organisms that float with the ocean's currents are a very important feeding source for fish. When plankton dies it has large impacts on fish populations.

This impact flows down the food chain with consequent impacts on our ability to purchase fish for dinner.

It's a similar story but with different consequences for the cane toad. The cane toad, which is native to South America was introduced in the 1930s in Far North Queensland (Australia). The plan was that it would help eradicate the native cane beetle that was destroying sugar cane crops. However, the introduction of a new player into the system had unintended consequences because there were no natural predators for the cane toad. So while the change solved one problem (the cane beetle), it also created a new problem (an increasing and spreading population of cane toads with resulting environmental damage across large parts of Australia). By not understanding the relationships and dynamics in the system, Australia was left with a large environmental issue, which it is still trying to cope with today.

This is what happens in systems – an event in one part of the system can have unintended consequences in another part.

The same process happens in organisations. An organisation may try to make a change in one part, only to find that it has consequences for another part of the organisation. This flow-on impact wasn't anticipated, nor was it identified as a potential concern when the change was being initially assessed. For example, management may be trying to change the culture of the organisation and they are making no progress because the actions being taken to alter it result in the system just self-correcting, and so no change is achieved.

Why does this happen?

Systems are complex, often ambiguous and highly connected. To work through a problem and to make changes in an organisation it's important to understand the system – how it works, what drives it, the points of connection and intersection, and how the parts interrelate to make the whole.

A system isn't linear. It's circular, with feedback loops and flows that can go in different directions. There are inputs, outputs, processes and outcomes. The distinguishing feature of a system is that if one part is removed or altered, the system is changed in some way.

Systems are often characterised by:

- **Ambiguity** – lots of information, ideas and changes, making it hard to grasp all the impacts.
- **Complexity** – a vast amount of change occurring simultaneously, the pace, nature and value of which continues to grow.
- **Connectedness** – everything is connected, but the connections are unknown and so impacts can go unseen and unaccounted for.
- **Diversity** – there are many different stakeholders (both internal and external to the organisation) with ideas, opinions, needs, and the desire to be heard.
- **Changeable** – systems don't remain static. The forces of change can be hard to understand because the normal cause and effect logic doesn't always operate in a system.

The point behind thinking and examining your organisation as a system is to take a broader perspective. What looks like the answer may not be the answer when you consider the impact on the whole organisation. What looks like the cause of the problem may not be the issue when you look at how the system is really operating.

KNOW THE SYSTEM

> "An organisation is a system, with a logic of its own, and all the weight of tradition and inertia. The deck is stacked in favour of the tried and proven ways of doing things and against the taking of risks and striking out in new directions."
>
> —John D. Rockefeller III, *The Second American Revolution*

If you want to be more influential you not only need to know yourself and understand others, but you need to understand the system in which you are working and how to leverage it. This is because one of the key criteria for organisational success is being able to get things done. Consequently, it's critical to know how to get change happening within the system. It's also important to understand the impact that the system is having on you and those around you.

Systems are hard to change, and it's likely you won't be able to change the way the system operates. What you can do is make sure you are best positioned to operate in the system and get traction and consequently progress.

STEP ONE: Know the context for change

The first step in understanding the system in which you are operating is understanding its nature. Systems are driven by change and inertia. It's often a case of push and pull, as different parts of the organisation's system work against each other.

Change is unavoidable, but the system will buck against it. The commonly used acronym is that today we live in a VUCA world: volatile, uncertain, complex and ambiguous. This VUCA world is shaped by technological, economic, competitive, environmental, political, regulatory, social and demographic changes.

Change is driven by some form of pressure. In nature, water is turned into steam by the pressure of heat. In societies, new laws are often passed due to pressure by the community. The same goes for organisations. There is some form of pressure that sparks the need for change – and that can be either internally or externally generated. External forces include competition, environment, social landscape, regulations and technology. While internal forces can include new leadership teams, cost pressures, mergers, changes in the organisation's life cycle and employee or cultural needs.

These forces don't happen in isolation from each other, and often a change is driven by multiple forces with differing impacts. Successful organisations always have an eye to the external environment and to understanding what is happening now and likely to be happening in the future. They know they can't stand still. If they do, they'll join the list of endangered or extinct companies. As Jack Welch said: *"When the rate of change inside an institution becomes slower than the rate of change outside, the end is in sight…"*.[32]

Every organisation will make a decision as to how they respond to those changes – what they do and don't do, when they'll do it, why they'll do it, and how they'll do it. It may mean changes to the organisation's strategy, structure or operating model, as well as to processes, roles, skills, capabilities, procedures, remuneration and culture. Change will create both disruption and opportunity – irrespective of whether the change is viewed positively or negatively by those impacted by it.

Understanding how change is initiated, designed, driven and executed in your organisation will help you better navigate the system and get things done. It will enable you to better position yourself to thrive through the change – both in terms of its impacts on you and, if you're in a leadership role, your team.

Additionally, if you are leading a change you need to know what to do to ensure the change is sustainable and achieves its desired benefits. To do that, it's important to understand the scale and nature of the change and respect the system into which the change is being introduced. Respect doesn't mean you like the way the system is working. It's acknowledging that you can't ignore the system and how it works if you want to be successful.

Identifying the type of change, helps you assess its size and scale and subsequently the potential impact. Organisational change comes in all shapes and sizes – small and incremental, transitional, and large and transformational:

- **Incremental adjustments** – change that happens in increments and small adjustments, and is quite linear and routine (i.e. process change).
- **Transitional** – change that involves moving from a clearly defined 'as is' to the 'to be' state, and the focus is on managing the transition from these two states (i.e. organisational restructure).
- **Transformational** – change that involves a fundamental reinvention of the organisation, which is more complex and challenging, and where the path to the future state is not clear. In this case, the change is more adaptive than technical and may involve an overhaul of the organisation's culture and business model.

The process to make change happen for these three types of change is different. Adjustments are relatively easy and can be managed through a typical base level change management program. They tend to be more a 'technical' rather than an 'adaptive' challenge.[33] That is, the issue is well understood, and therefore the solution is relatively easy to find. Changes of this type can be more linear in nature, and are less complex and ambiguous.

Drawing on the work of William Bridges, transitional-type change requires a more sophisticated level of planning and a heightened awareness of the impact on people.[34] In this type of change it is necessary to understand what is ending, what the future state will look like, and how to manage through the 'middle' of the change. This is what Bridges calls the neutral zone. It is called a neutral zone because it is during this phase that employees can often feel lost. They're not at the end or the start of the new operating environment, and they can feel bewildered about what to do.

Changes of this type can involve a mixture of technical or adaptive problems. An adaptive challenge is harder to define, and finding the solution isn't easy as there is typically no one right answer, and the best approach can be hard to find and counterintuitive. It becomes important to understand what type of problem is being faced, as the approach to address it can be quite different.

At the other end of the spectrum are transformations. These days the term transformation is over-used. Many change programs that are called a 'transformation' are in fact a transitional program. A true transformation is when the organisation is completely changing – from the inside to the outside. It is therefore far more complex and difficult to navigate and steer to a successful conclusion. Transformations involve numerous adaptive challenges. Unfortunately, many organisations that embark on a transformation don't make a lot of progress as they fail to recognise and respond to those challenges.

Transformations can take many years, and the journey is often hard to navigate and very difficult to fully plan. This is well documented and backed up by research from eminent researchers in this field.

Anand and Barsoux who examined a number of large-scale transformations to understand the ingredients for success were two such researchers. They found that *"Transformation journeys cannot be mapped out entirely in advance. As leaders, we must steer a course between order and disorder at the same time, leaving room for experimentation and divergent views, while simultaneously providing boundaries and key ideas so that the energy can be channelled".* [35]

A key part of this analysis is being clear on what is driving the change. The forces can be both externally and internally driven. For example:

- **External forces include** – changes in customer demands and expectations; new entrants to the market; changing competitive forces; alterations in the social landscape; and new technology, etc.
- **Internal forces include** – changes in leadership; a need to alter organisational culture or brand; cost and revenue drivers; new opportunities; changes in the organisational life cycle; mergers and acquisitions; and new technology systems, etc.

Knowing which drivers are at play helps you position the change and the reason for the change. Also, while generalisations can be dangerous, experience has shown me that change is usually easier if the organisation has initiated the change, in contrast to when disruptive and adaptive change is forced on an organisation. In the latter case, the organisation is often scrambling to make progress, after many years of ignoring the fact that their industry is changing and they should respond and adapt to it.

The level of planning, involvement and challenge will be different for each type of change.

☑ CHECKPOINT ACTIVITY

Think about an organisational change you are involved with and ask yourself:

- ☐ Is the change incremental, transitional or transformational?
- ☐ Has it been driven by internal or external needs?

- ☐ Is it planned (proactive) or forced (reactive) upon the organisation?
- ☐ Is the change the result of disruptive forces in the market?
- ☐ Is the change an adaptive or technical challenge?

Answering these questions will help you understand the driving forces for the change, and the type of change your organisation is about to embark on. The next logical step is to understand the culture in which these changes are trying to be implemented.

STEP TWO: Examine the culture

It's almost impossible to make change in an organisation without understanding the cultural system in which you are working. Culture permeates everything that happens in an organisation. Hazardous cultures produce hazardous results. In cultures where questioning isn't welcome and where leaders don't listen, the environment is ripe for poor decision-making and outcomes.

I've worked with leaders who through their autocratic leadership style created a climate of fear. This fed into the organisation's culture. People were scared to speak up. They were intimidated and uncomfortable to challenge and question authority. As a result, issues went underground, only to surface later with greater consequences.

Culture influences how we think and behave. One of the world's leading experts on culture, Edgar Schein, defines it as:

"Culture is a pattern of shared basic assumptions that was learned by a group as it solved its problems of external adaptation and internal integration, that has worked well enough to be considered valid, and therefore, to be taught to new members as the correct way to perceive, think and feel in relation to those problems".[36]

People commonly talk about culture as the way things are done around here. It is the unwritten rules of behaviour about what is acceptable and not acceptable.

Culture influences incredibly quickly. When you enter a new work environment you quickly learn the accepted way to behave. Behaviour that is off-culture is shunned and ridiculed. We see this at play in the animal kingdom as well.

In the early 1970s, a primatologist – Hans Kummer – was working in Ethiopia with two species of baboons. The first species were Savanna baboons which live in large troops. The other species were Hamadryas baboons which have a more complex and multi-level society. When confronted with a threatening male the females of the two species reacted differently: a Hamadryas baboon placated the male by approaching him, whereas a Savanna baboon would run away to avoid injury. Kummer took a female from each group and released them into the alternate tribe. What he found was that initially these two females carried out their species-typical behaviour. But, it didn't take long for them to be socialised to the new way of behaving. In fact, it took around an hour.[37]

This is the process of what I call "culturalisation" and it happens to all of us. If you remember back to your first day at work, you would have very quickly picked up on the required social cues and behaviours. If you committed a social faux pas, someone would have either pulled you aside to say something or you would have got strange looks from people. As tribal creatures we can easily shun people who don't conform to and adopt the conventional way of behaving. If people do something that is different to everyone else, they can quickly be labelled as 'odd'. This is culture at work. It is critical to be aware of it because when you are 'in the culture' you often don't notice how the culture is playing out – both positively and negatively. To you it is just normal behaviour.

An organisation's culture comes with labels. A culture can be described as agile, toxic, lazy, innovative and progressive, for example. Often multiple words will be used to describe an organisation's culture. In large organisations, there will also typically be a dominant culture that pervades the organisation and then many sub-cultures across the organisation.

I've seen organisations where the over-arching culture was competitive, aggressive and bureaucratic, and yet individual teams were able to work around that and provide wonderful examples of team work, collaboration and compassionate behaviour. They specifically chose to operate in a different way when they worked together.

Culture is created through a number of elements. These can be broken into soft and hard factors:

- **Soft levers** include the leadership behaviours, plus norms, rituals and symbols. They are often the elements that seem less tangible and harder to pinpoint.
- **Hard levers** are the organisation's operating model and organisational design, stated values, policies and processes. These elements are often the items that are written down and codified in some way.

As a leader (or an aspiring leader) it's critical to understand the cultural dynamics in which you are working – what they mean and the impact they have on how you, your team and how those around you operate. Is the organisation focused on 'profit at all costs'? Is its philosophy based on sustainable returns? Is the leadership authentic and exemplary? Or is it command and control?

☑ CHECKPOINT ACTIVITY

To uncover the nature of your organisation's culture you can gather insights by asking your team members and peers the following questions:

☐ What do you like and not like about the current culture?

☐ What do you observe when you look at the behaviour of the leadership team? Do they act consistently? Are they living up to the stated organisational values and behaviours?

- [ ] What are the organisation's rituals, customs, traditions and norms? When are they on display and how frequently?
- [ ] Does the organisation have a written vision and values statement and is it something that is held up as important and seen as inspirational by people at all hierarchical levels?
- [ ] Are there consequences if people don't live up to the organisation's stated values?
- [ ] What are the rules of the game both written (i.e. policies, procedures and guidelines) and unwritten (i.e. expectations, rituals, etc.) and how are they implemented and enforced?
- [ ] How does the organisation's operating model and organisation design (i.e. structure, governance, decision rights, accountability standards, performance management approach) impact the culture?
- [ ] Does the workplace and its physical space (i.e. offices versus open plan) help or hinder the culture? In what way?
- [ ] What stories are told about the organisation and its leaders? What stories are told inside and outside the work environment, and how do they differ?
- [ ] How do the organisation's formal communication channels operate? Are they effective? Do they enable two-way feedback and communication?
- [ ] How is information formally and informally shared through the organisation? Which channels are more effective and do you need to rely on the 'grapevine' to find out what is going on?
- [ ] Are you proud to work for this organisation, and would you recommend it to your friends and family?
- [ ] Does the organisation hire and promote based on cultural fit and suitability?

Answering those questions will go a long way to help you uncover the nature of your organisation's culture and its impact on how your organisation operates and what can impede or accelerate progress.

STEP THREE: Anchor your power base

The role that leaders play in setting the organisation's culture is well documented. When assessing your organisation's change leadership think about it from two perspectives: what criteria are leaders using to make decisions; and how are they leading change?

This model is black and white and in reality organisations and people operate on a continuum. However, for illustration purposes, it's helpful to be definitive.

The decision focus is either: good corporate citizen where there is a sustainable balance between risk, return, profits and contribution to the community, or it is the minimum and profit at all costs.

Leadership can either be exemplar, where behaviour is role-modelled on best practice and what is needed in the circumstances, or it is the antithesis where leadership is absent and self-serving.

Figure 14: Conscious change leader approach

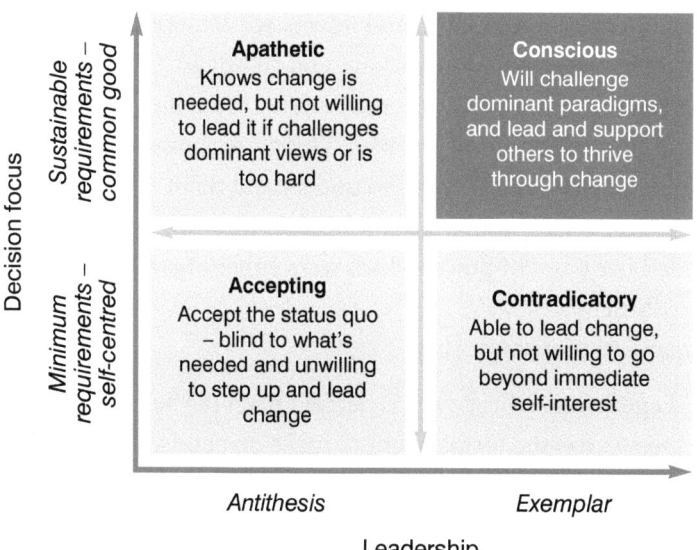

An accepting change leader is one who does the bare minimum on all levels. He or she is not prepared to rock the boat or challenge the status quo. They accept the situation for what it is. An apathetic change leader is someone who knows the right thing to do and how to do it but can't be bothered, or lacks the courage to step up. A contradictory change leader is one who espouses all the right type of leadership values and behaviours but doesn't carry this through in terms of how they make decisions, treat people and lead change.

A conscious change leader, which is what I hope you are aspiring to be, is one who is willing to challenge the status quo and to strive for great, sustainable decisions and outcomes. Conscious leaders do this in a way that exemplifies good leadership.

As a conscious leader you know how to build and use a power base wisely. You lead with your heart, as well as your head. All organisations have power bases. Those power bases are based on different forces. If you are to have influence in a system you need to understand these power bases and how to work them.

Power has negative connotations, and rightly so. Often power is wielded as a force for evil, not good. Power is the ability to get someone else to do something for you. There are, however, different sources of power and it's useful to understand them.

In 1959, social psychologists John French and Bertram Raven identified five bases of power which were either organisationally or personally derived.[38]

Organisational power is:

- **Legitimate** – this power is derived from the belief that a person has the formal right to make demands, and to expect those around them to accept them. You will have heard the term 'formal authority' before. This is the same concept. It exists because of the person's role in the organisation.

- **Reward-based** – this power arises from a person's ability to provide rewards that someone else wants.
- **Coercive** – this power, which is the opposite of reward-based, comes from the belief that a person can punish (or threaten) others for not doing something. This may be the loss of a job or an entitlement.

Personal power is:

- **Reverent** – this arises when a person is revered, trusted or looked up to. This type of power is the result of the person's perceived attractiveness, value or charisma.
- **Expert** – this power is based on a person's knowledge and skills. For example, doctors usually have expert power because their role and knowledge places them in a position of trust and influence.

In your organisation you will see these types of power playing out. The question for you is how much power do you have? What type of power base do you rely on? How do you use it? Do you use it wisely?

Knowing the type of leader that you want to be – a conscious leader – how can you achieve that and use power wisely?

These are important questions to reflect on. I've seen people in organisations unknowingly give away their power. I've seen others use their power for their own vain purposes and agenda. I've also seen people use their power to promote and achieve better outcomes.

How you leverage the power you have goes a long way to defining the type of leader you are now and will be into the future.

If you want to be a conscious change leader then anchor your power to a noble purpose, and know how and when to use it wisely.

WORK THE SYSTEM

> "It should be borne in mind that there is nothing more difficult to arrange, more doubtful of success, and more dangerous to carry through than initiating change… The innovator makes enemies of all those who prospered under the old order and only lukewarm support is forthcoming from those who will prosper under the new."
>
> —Machiavelli, "The Prince" (1532)

Every day we hear how we are living in an increasingly interconnected and digitally-disrupted world. These connections create complexity and ambiguity, but they also offer amazing opportunities and challenges for organisations and the people who work in them. From my perspective, this pace of change is incredibly exciting.

Sadly, organisational change efforts are littered with failures. Having worked in large-scale organisational change programs, I've witnessed these failures play out. If you want to 'work the system' you need to understand what can hold you back from successful change. The failure can never be pinpointed to one reason.

The key culprits include:

- Having a too-cautious management culture and executives who don't support the change or role-model the right behaviours. This includes executive teams not spending enough time leading the change.
- Taking a business-as-usual approach to the change, such that the changes are not effectively planned or prioritised, and the scope is unclear and focus is lost.

- Not painting a picture of the future so there is no clarity on how all the changes that are taking place connect with where the organisation is going. Consequently, the change is seen as isolated from the organisation's strategic direction.
- Failing to account for the system in which the change is occurring, and therefore not addressing the interconnections and dependencies that exist.
- Lacking an organisation-wide approach to change, so there is no common language, governance or program and change management methodology.
- Taking too long to show that the change is working, not being agile in delivery, and expecting the changes to be linear and perfectly sequenced.
- Ignoring the culture change required to support the change and assuming that culture doesn't matter.
- Having an organisational history of failed changes, and this change is seen as the 'next shiny new toy' so the employees don't take it seriously.
- Limited understanding of the organisation's capability and capacity to change, along with no roadmap to show the sequence of the changes, or assessment of the organisation's change maturity.
- Setting a volume and pace of change that's unrealistic for employees to absorb at the same time.
- Not enough investment in building the skills and capabilities of employees to thrive through the change.

STEP ONE: Keep it real

To make change happen in an organisation it's important to be realistic about the challenges you will face. I often use the terms ready, willing and able, because to achieve successful organisational change the organisation and its people need to be ready, willing and able to change.

- **Ready to change** – the organisation knows where it wants to get to and has a well-constructed plan for execution, with a logically and thoughtfully sequenced change roadmap. There are always unknowns when kicking off a change, so you can't plan for everything. You can, however, ensure that your organisation is ready to be flexible and adaptive as it goes through the change. This way it can take advantage of opportunities and respond swiftly to issues as they arise.

- **Willing to change** – the organisation has effective leadership and the roles and responsibilities of the change sponsor, project team and leaders are clear, and they are willing to step up and lead the change. This is imperative. Changes are much harder if the alignment between strategic intent and the leaders' actions is absent. Progress will suffer too if accountability is unclear.

- **Able to change** – the organisation has the capacity and capability to execute the change and is able to invest the resources to ensure that impacted stakeholders are well prepared for the change. The organisation needs to devote both financial and people resources to ensuring that those impacted by the change are not only able to cope with it but know what is expected of them and have the behavioural and technical skills to thrive through it.

These elements help to create the tipping point for organisational change. This tipping point can go one of two ways – up or down! Many of you will know Malcolm Gladwell's concept of the tipping point. He talks about a tipping point as that moment when an idea, trend or social behaviour crosses a threshold, such that it spreads exponentially.[39]

In organisations there are tipping points for change too. These tipping points occur at two ends of the scale. At one end of the scale, there are tipping points in which organisational change reaches a critical mass, where it has achieved buy-in and acceptance from stakeholders and end-users.

At the other end of the scale, there is organisational change where people are so overwhelmed by the scale, frequency and pace of change that there is no buy-in or acceptance. Consequently, not only does the change initiative fail but the organisation can become paralysed with indecision and inertia, and experience a spike in employee and customer dissatisfaction.

Securing change acceptance can be hard and it's made even harder when an organisation's ambitious change agenda does not take into account the culture, capacity or capability of the organisation to adopt the change.

Time and time again I've seen Project or Investment Committees agree on a long list of projects for the organisation to deliver. The Committee will examine the projects in terms of the cost to deliver and expected benefits, but it won't examine whether the organisation is ready, willing and able to cope with the change. Knowing the totality of change occurring across the organisation, what capability gaps exist in delivery and end-user adoption, and how to best sequence the change so that the impacts are well managed is critical.

Instead, what usually happens is there are multiple change programs occurring at the same time, often impacting the same group of people. This creates confusion, particularly when the implementation efforts are disconnected from each other. What the end-users see is a barrage of changes coming down the pipeline but little information as to how the changes connect back to the organisation's strategic agenda, and what it means for them holistically.

Plus, there's usually limited impact analysis on how these changes will play out in the system, and what changes to the culture are required to support and enhance the change execution and sustainability of benefits.

☑ CHECKPOINT ACTIVITY

As a starting point, if your organisation is going through a change there are some fundamental issues to investigate. To find out how ready, willing and able your organisation is to change investigate the following items:

- [ ] The size, scale and nature of your change initiatives – find out how many initiatives are 'in flight' (that is, projects that are already under way) or about to be started. At a minimum, the project portfolio list should detail the initiatives, their cost, stage gates, who the sponsor is, key milestones, and the intended benefits.
- [ ] Know how the proposed changes will impact the business – so you can identify what areas of the business are being impacted, when, to what extent and in what way. This impact assessment process enables you to critically examine whether those areas have the capacity and capability to cope with the changes planned. This assessment should result in the construction of an integrated map of all change initiatives so the hot spots (i.e. those business areas with multiple change impacts at the same time) can be identified.
- [ ] Identify who will benefit from the change. Stakeholders and employees will be impacted in different ways because of the change. Knowing who will gain or not gain from the change is useful as it helps you understand the potential reasons for their response and behaviour. Once you understand their position it becomes easier to address. Also, identify the supporters and detractors of the change – both internal and external to the organisation. It is important to think beyond traditional networks and hierarchies in this regard.
- [ ] Identify the benefits to be delivered from the initiative. This is essential and yet it is often only considered as part of the

business-case development. Even then, the level of attention given to it is often less than optimal. If you don't understand the benefits, and don't have an agreed way of monitoring their delivery, it's almost impossible to know how successful (or otherwise) the project has been. Identifying and monitoring benefits starts from day 1. The project list should identify when benefits are expected to start accruing and who is accountable for delivering them, along with the expected return on investment (and over what time period).

☐ Look at changes or projects that are already underway, and articulate the gap between planned and actual (or newly assessed) benefit delivery from those initiatives. The point of this assessment is to examine the list of 'in flight' projects against the original benefits estimate. From there you can determine what's driven the gap between the original benefit delivery and the new benefit delivery. This will provide learnings for your planning, and may also indicate that a current project should not be continued.

☐ Craft the sequence and delivery schedule of the proposed changes so you can determine the best delivery approach. This involves examining whether the program of work is sequenced in a way that is logical and accounts for the organisation's capacity to absorb and adopt the change. Based on these insights the delivery schedule for some initiatives may need to be altered.

☐ Be aware of potential roadblocks that may arise. Knowing where you may come up against obstacles that will hinder the successful implementation of the proposed changes means you can anticipate and respond quickly. This process may include: identifying where there may be gaps in resources which may impact delivery timeframes; reviewing the stakeholder analysis to see if there are advocates for the change, or too many blockers; and examining the delivery risks that exist during the project and the risks that may arise when the change is in place. These details will help provide an accurate picture of each initiative and the likelihood of delivering it on time, on budget and to quality, and with end-user and stakeholder acceptance.

I also recommend at the outset to undertake a realistic assessment of the potential risks that may arise. This change risk assessment helps you understand the organisation's current state and issues that may arise to impede the change or transformation. When you understand the risks, it's easier to put in place plans to minimise the likelihood that they will eventuate and minimise the impact if they do. You'll also have a much more realistic assessment of the challenges you may encounter.

This approach also helps you be better prepared in the event that an issue arises. Experience shows that contingency planning enables people to cope better and the issue is better managed. Once you understand the risks you can establish appropriate early warning indicators to monitor them and provide an alert or trigger to do something if it looks like an issue is about to happen.

These are important considerations as understanding these factors will help you better plan, stage and sequence your roadmap of change initiatives and also know where to focus capability uplift activities. This might sound overly simplified, but experience has shown that it is often the simple things that make a real difference to how a change is experienced and the likelihood of the expected benefits being delivered. This approach is not about creating an inflexible plan. It is about having a strong sense of direction and clarity on the way ahead.

These suggested activities help ensure you are 'keeping it real' by having a realistic assessment of the change, clarity on the strategic direction and knowledge on how the program can be best approached for success and to secure the desired benefits.

STEP TWO: Lead with purpose

Teams are brought together to get things done. Consequently, having a common purpose and clarity on what the team needs to achieve together is crucial. Unfortunately, this doesn't always exist. I'm amazed at the number of times team members tell me they don't know why their role is part of a particular team, and they don't know what other team members do.

Sometimes this lack of clarity is the result of a recent restructure, where two teams have been merged into one team. The newly combined team's purpose isn't clear, nor is the role that each team member needs to play as this is still being worked through. Other times it exists because the leader has simply failed to make it clear. This ambiguity breeds disconnect and distrust.

For teams to work together effectively it's essential that they have clarity of purpose. That clarity, combined with commitment to delivering on it, helps you and your colleagues sustain focus when progress is slow.

Creating a shared vision with the team can really help. This is a vision that everyone is committed to bringing to life. When I started my business, I created a vision board that helped clarify the goals to achieve over the years. I stuck it on the wall above my desk so that I looked at it every day. It became a point of focus when things got tough. If a proposal for work got rejected by a potential client I would look at the vision board and it would inspire me to keep going. This helped me maintain perspective and focus. While this story centres on a personal vision, it easily translates into a bigger context. Having a big picture perspective is important for people. They want to know that what they do at work matters – that their work contributes in some way to the organisation's success.

Being able to lead with purpose also means you are equipped and motivated to lead people through change. If you want to be a conscious leader this cannot be outsourced to someone else. Leadership is essential as the change needs to be driven by the leader and you need to have the confidence and accountability to take this on.

It helps if you are aware of what's in front of you and realistic about what you are stepping in to.

Humans have a common ability to be overly optimistic, particularly when it comes to large-scale change. Often with the best of intent, we over-estimate what can get done, in what timeframe, and with what level of resources. Problems or roadblocks remain hidden or dormant and then arise at the most inconvenient time. This makes it much harder to solve issues and get traction than originally thought.

To compound things, the environment in which you are working doesn't remain static as you are making change. It keeps changing and so there is the complexity of 'change on change' occurring. People often become demotivated when things get hard and progress is slow. Plus, different stakeholders in the system have alternate and competing goals. This means that success for one stakeholder can come at the expense of the other.

Additionally, when projects are initiated there are many unknowns. As these unknowns become knowns, what can and can't be achieved (in the timeframe and with the allocated resources) becomes clearer. This too can lead to changes in the delivery approach and timing.

All of this can easily cause you (and those around you) to lose motivation. However, it is easier to stay the course if your purpose is clear.

Organisations are big systems, and from my experience, making change in them is possible. Here are some tips to keep you on track when the change gets tough and you feel like you are not making progress:

- Be realistic – don't underestimate the complexity and internal resistance that you will face. Understand it. Prepare for it. Work with it.

- There are many moving parts in an organisation and you need a well-coordinated suite of change activities. You need to understand how this change connects with, or is dependent on, other changes going on in the organisation.
- Executives expect results – be careful about over-promising and under-delivering. Know where your efforts will produce the greatest results. Know your points of leverage and be sure to deliver quick wins so you can show results early and regularly throughout the change.
- You cannot be a 'one-man-band' – you need the right people involved and the executives lined up and on board. In a transformation, the organisation's executive team should be devoting more than 50% of their time to the transformation. You need the right team around you, so if you make hiring mistakes fix them quickly.
- Be courageous – don't be scared to try something new. Whichever path you take you will make mistakes. Fail fast. Admit them, fix them and move on. Don't get stuck in gridlock.
- Be well planned – a poorly planned execution roadmap will lead to distractions, wasted energy and resources and under-delivering.
- Understand the organisational system – the context, culture, structural inertia and bias that exists. While you may not be able to change these elements to suit your needs, greater awareness will help you know the best approach to take to minimise their impact.
- Be flexible and adaptive – as you move through the change and progress you will uncover different challenges, constraints and priorities which may necessitate a different approach.

- Expect that things will go wrong – change and transformations are complex and there are many unknowns at the beginning. It's critical to have a realistic assessment of the potential issues that may arise. The leadership and team working on the change must be alert to the warning signs of issues and a contingency approach should be in place to address them if they eventuate.

Above all else, don't lose sight of why you are doing this. Keep focused on your purpose.

STEP THREE: Leverage all angles

There's no doubt that culture is bigger than one person. However, regardless of your role you can have a degree of influence on the organisation's culture. You are not only in the culture and influenced by it, but you are part of the influencing forces in the culture. The span of that influence may be narrow or wide, deep or shallow.

Start by identifying what cultural forces can impede or stop progress being made. This requires you to be realistic about the type of culture you are working in and what is possible.

> **STEP UP TIP**
> You can use the questions detailed in the section on examining the culture in Chapter 5 (see pages 119 to 120) to assess what type of culture you are working with.

It's also helpful to accept that there will be some things you can change and others you can't. It's important to know the difference so you don't waste time and energy on things outside your control.

I've often used the Stephen Covey diagram of Circle of Influence and Circle of Concern. This process helps target your attention to those issues that you can influence. There is no point worrying about things outside your control. You can be concerned, but if you can't influence the outcome there's no point expending energy trying to change it. It's a very useful way of sorting through and prioritising your attention and efforts.

For example, you are less likely to be able to influence organisationally based cultural levers. These include: remuneration and reward structures, policies, alignment of the operating model to the desired culture, and how information flows through the organisation. However, you can influence individually based levers which focus more on how you motivate, empower and inspire those around you.

If you want to influence the culture you need to start with yourself and ensure your behaviour is in line with expectations. If you're leading a team, they will be looking to you for guidance and for 'tone from the top'. Colleagues will also look at your behaviour and from that make an assessment of your character and leadership potential.

Your leadership style is critical as it has a huge impact on the culture directly around you. If you are a leader there is a lot you can do to make your team more productive and engaged. Consider how you make decisions and share information. The more collaborative you are, the greater involvement and support you will get from your team. Do you make decisions collaboratively, directionally or dictatorially?

How you make decisions can be influenced by circumstances. There is a time and place for each style. During a crisis, a dictatorial approach (i.e. where one person makes the decision) can be best. However, when you want high engagement, a collaborative decision process is best. The point is to be conscious of the process you are using.

Also consider how you share information with your team and colleagues and make sure they have all the information and knowledge they need to do their job well. Effective leaders provide information which is timely, fact-based and purposeful. They're not a roadblock. They also provide relevant and timely feedback. People want to know how they are going. To be useful, the feedback should be authentic, compassionate and based on a real desire to support and encourage the person's personal development.

Seek to understand your team members – their mindset, interests and goals. Be clear on your team's purpose and how you work together to achieve common objectives. Also, make sure you hire people for cultural fit, not just technical skills. It's also critical to be honest with yourself about how you treat people. Is everyone treated fairly or do you play favourites? People are acutely attuned to unfairness and will see immediately if you treat people differently.

The best leaders back their teams and ensure the team members know they're supported. This support is fundamental, particularly in highly charged political work places. Teams that are 'backed' feel more empowered to get things done and more comfortable taking risks.

Above all else, if you want to be able to 'work the system' then behave consistently and authentically as a conscious change leader. Being comfortable to do that is a real sign that you have influence.

6. Appeal to human insight

> "…What will separate the leaders of tomorrow from the leaders of today will be their ability to manage change and to understand the world, not only as it is but as it may soon be…"
>
> —*Winston Churchill on his 75th birthday in 1949*

When you are working in an organisation you cannot be an island. You must be able to work with other people to get things done. Conscious leaders know how to get things done through people. They have the ability to motivate, encourage and inspire people to action. While it is debated as to how much of these leadership traits are inherent versus learned, I work from the premise that they can be learned. To do that it's necessary to understand people and what motivates them.

I've been very fortunate in my career to have worked with some brilliant leaders and some not so brilliant leaders. From each of them

I took away learnings. From the brilliant leaders I learned the power of compassion, authenticity and enabling each team member to be their best. These leaders didn't shy away from showing who they were. They shared experiences and were genuinely interested in my experiences and what I had to offer. They nurtured my interest and love of a challenge and encouraged me to take leaps into the unknown. These leaps into roles I had never done before felt safe because I knew they had my back. They were leaders who over time became mentors. I still rely on many of them today for advice.

From the not so brilliant leaders, I learned the importance of listening and taking the time to understand what motivates your team. These leaders all had exceptional talents in many areas, but they failed to inspire those around them. In some cases, they wielded power unnecessarily. In other cases, they failed to empower the team and prevaricated over decisions. Interestingly, often they could theorise the importance of behaviours and leadership, but those theories weren't put into practice. These deficiencies held them back from being as successful as they could have been.

Over the years, I've been fascinated to unpick those behavioural insights and to understand in greater depth what drove that behaviour. Helping me understand the motivations of others made it easier for me to accept the seemingly irrational behaviour. I've found that the more I understood people the easier it was to work with them. Being curious about what motivated them made me less judgmental. As well, trying to see things from their perspective helped me be more reasonable. I can't say I always pulled this off, but I tried.

Organisations can feel soul-less and heartless, and consequently can be really tough environments to work in. It doesn't need to be like that. If there were more leaders leading from a base of insight and integrity our workplaces would be much healthier and happier.

I am encouraging you to take the time to build insight-based relationships that are happy, healthy and well balanced. It is with insight-based relationships that you will be able to encourage and support change. It is through these relationships that you will be able to activate, leverage and sustain a platform for influence.

There are three core building blocks to achieving this: nature, narrative and nurture (see Figure 15).

Figure 15: Building insight-based relationships

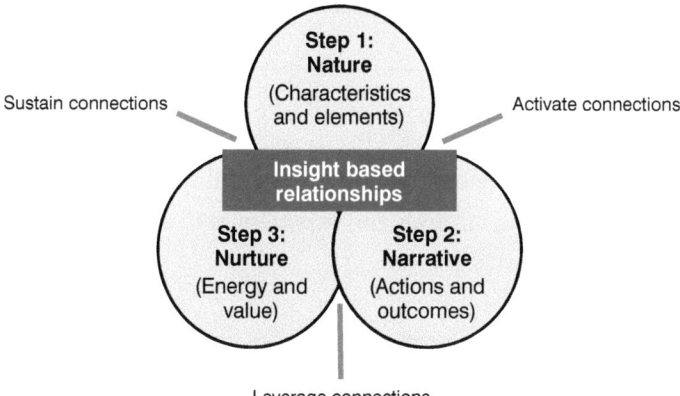

Nature is about understanding the fundamental dynamics of human interaction and what motivates people to behave the way they do. This is the foundational building block. Once you understand this element it is easier to build effective relationships.

That takes you to the second element – narrative. This is about taking what you've learned about people and putting it into action. It's about how you lead people, and help and guide them through change.

The last element is how you can successfully nurture relationships. It is best to take a long-term view of relationships – viewing all of them as worthwhile. There are times to walk away from relationships that are unhealthy, but generally most relationships have something to offer. Typically, the more you invest in the relationship, the more you will gain.

Having insight-based relationships will help you:

- Motivate your team members and those around you to high performance.
- Persuade people to hear your point of view.
- Get things done by collaborating successfully with people – some of whom you'll naturally 'click with' and others with whom you won't.
- Position yourself effectively and communicate with people at all organisational levels.
- Work more effectively with people of different backgrounds, cultures and experiences to enable change and make progress.

THE NATURE OF MOTIVATION

> "Change is a threat when done to me, but an opportunity when done by me."
>
> *Professor Rosabeth Moss Kanter,*
> *Harvard Business School*

In the first half of this book you gained insights into yourself. It's now time to gain insights into other people and how they are motivated to think, act and react. This is about understanding the nature of people so you can motivate with knowledge and make progress during times of change.

STEP ONE: Motivate with knowledge

There are countless motivation theories which espouse different views on what motivates people. For example, a psychodynamic approach looks at the differences between conscious and unconscious motives. A behaviourist perspective asserts that humans repeat behaviours that secure rewards and avoid those that lead to punishment. While the cognitive approach offers that people perform behaviours that they value and can attain.[40]

I'm not going to touch on all the motivational theories but it is useful to draw on some of the most well-known to set the context.

One of the earliest motivational theories was put forward by Abraham Maslow, who in the 1940s constructed his theory of needs. This theory is classified as a humanistic approach and explains that all human beings have basic needs. As people have a lower need met, they strive to have the next need met. And so humans strive to move from meeting physiological needs, safety needs, the need for love and belonging, and the need for self-esteem through to self-actualisation. While the approach was never scientifically validated and has many detractors, it provides a useful perspective. Everyone has needs, and typically the more they're met the greater a person's satisfaction level.

Building on this work, David McClelland identified three motivators that he believed we all have: a need for achievement (i.e. making progress, getting outcomes); affiliation (i.e. a need to belong and be liked); or power (i.e. a need to control or dominate). He argued that people will have different characteristics depending on what is their dominant motivator.

Shortly thereafter, Vroom released his expectancy theory which assumed that behaviour resulted from conscious choices, with the purpose being to maximise pleasure and minimise pain. Around the same time, Frederick Herzberg developed his two factor theory which stated that there are certain elements in a workplace that can motivate, and a different set of elements that can de-motivate. He believed that these elements were mutually exclusive. He referred to the demotivators (i.e. pay, company policy, supervision quality, working conditions, status, etc.) as 'hygiene factors'. While the motivators (i.e. achievement, recognition, responsibility, advancement, learning) were labelled as 'motivating factors'. The logic is that people expect the hygiene factors to be in place when they accept a job. If they're not, they are quickly dissatisfied. It is the motivating elements that encourage a person to go above and beyond in their job.

These theories and the many others that exist offer a perspective on how people are motivated. What they also show is that people are motivated in many different ways and by different things. Some people are easily motivated others less so. Importantly, there is much we are still learning in this field.

Sadly, despite the fact there are countless motivational theories, organisations are still failing to put in place the fundamental elements to motivate people in the workplace. This isn't to say they aren't trying. Some are, but many are still just paying lip service to the concept of staff engagement.

When I look back to my time working in large corporates it was easy to see the leaders who motivated their teams and those who didn't. The leaders who motivated, quite simply, led. They led with compassion, support, understanding and care. They set a clear vision; behaved consistently and fairly; backed their team members and supported them; encouraged them to do their best; and empowered them to act. In many respects the actions undertaken were relatively simple. They said hello every day. They asked you about yourself and your interests. They took an interest in your work and your personal life. They returned phone calls and gave you feedback on your work. They treated you as an equal and listened to your point of view.

These leaders were also able to overcome some of the organisational rigidity and barriers that made engagement and motivation harder. In return, they created teams with real energy and purpose and as result, made enormous progress.

In contrast, the leaders who didn't motivate led by wielding power and authority. They weren't interested in you unless it was about what you could do for them. They were incredibly self-centred and egotistical.

I remember one senior leader who never said hello to anyone when he came into the office. I always recall the time we had Christmas drinks and everyone on the floor came together to celebrate. He introduced himself to this young guy as if he had never seen him before. This guy sat two metres away from his desk. But, this executive was so consumed with himself that he could walk past that person's desk every working day for six months and not notice him. It spoke volumes to me about his character.

This was the same person who when I went to Brisbane for my grandmother's funeral expressed no compassion or sadness for my family's loss. Despite knowing where I had been, his only question when I came back into the office was: "Where have you been?" My response: "At my grandmother's funeral". His response: "What took you so long?"

As a leader, there are some things you can change and other things you can't change in an organisation. It's important to know the difference. For example, you may not be able to change how the organisation's remuneration and reward system is structured as you may not be senior enough to influence this. But, you may be able to influence how the rewards are allocated amongst your team. You can also take the time to understand how your team is feeling, which is why it's important to understand the difference between intrinsic and extrinsic motivation.

Originally, the belief was that motivating people in an organisational context was about reward and punishment. This approach was based on agency theory. It operated from the premise that organisations are collections of individuals each trying to maximise their own self-interest. Managers are the agents and shareholders are the principals. Under this theory, problems arise because there are different desires or goals between the principal and agent. For example, they may have different comfort levels with regard to the amount of risk the company takes on, or different financial objectives. You see this play out in real life when executives take actions that aren't in the shareholders' interests. For instance, when they use company funds for personal expenses.

Pay-for-performance systems, which operate in many organisations, were an attempt to minimise agency theory. They were introduced to get the people who worked in the organisation to do what those who owned it wanted them to do. However, the research shows that such systems have unintended consequences.

Dating back to the 1970s, psychologist Edward Deci ran an experiment showing how incentivising students with money to solve puzzles actually made them less interested in working on them after being paid.[41] The group of students who hadn't been offered money worked on the puzzles longer and with more interest. Jeffrey Pfeffer, a Stanford academic, found that focusing on compensation diminishes teamwork, causes people to focus too much on short-term goals and encourages political behaviour, such as 'managing up'.[42]

Similarly, Dan Ariely, a researcher in behavioural economics, ran an experiment in India looking at the impact of bonuses on performance. He found that performance was lowest when the bonus was highest. He repeated the experiment in the United States and found the same result. He concluded that the stress caused by what was seen as 'high stakes' – when the money was high – resulted in over attention to the bonus, as opposed to the task itself. And this affected behaviour.[43]

Deci's work uncovered the difference between extrinsic and intrinsic motivation. Extrinsic motivation is the kind that comes from outside sources, such as pay, bonuses and punishment. When the motivation is extrinsic you are being motivated to behave in a certain way to either secure a reward or to avoid punishment. Whereas intrinsic motivation is the motivation that comes from within yourself. It is much more sustaining because you are doing the thing for yourself – the reward is the action itself. Understanding the difference between the two motivational types and how and when to use them is an important technique to consider.

> **STEP UP TIP**
> As a leader, while you may not be able to control the extrinsic motivational factors in your work environment, you can certainly play a key role in providing the essential elements needed to support the intrinsic motivational factors coming to the fore.

Rather than using the 'carrot and stick' approach consider how you can build engagement by creating a sense of common purpose and cooperation. This is backed up by research which reveals that our brain produces higher levels of dopamine when we are in a positive environment. Dopamine is like a natural drug that is released by the brain. There is growing research which shows that people experiencing 'positive' emotions are able to create more options when solving problems, collaborate better and generally perform better at work.

This doesn't mean you ignore pay structures all together. Because while pay may not be the ultimate motivator, it can certainly be a demotivator. People compare themselves to others in terms of outcomes (benefits and rewards) and inputs (effort, time expended, skill level and ability). I've worked in organisations where people were told not to talk about their salary and benefits with their co-workers but of course they did. It's natural to compare yourself to other people. People don't want to be unfairly treated. If a person believes they work harder than someone else, and yet they are paid less, they'll be unhappy. While we would commonly see this as fairness, in research terms it is known as equity theory.

As Furnham and Taylor note: *"Equity theory is concerned with outcomes and inputs as they are perceived by the people involved, not as they actually are".*[44] What happens in practice is that the greater the perceived inequity, the greater the motivation for the person to try and find a way to restore the balance. How they do this will vary, but it can lead to an employee being less productive, taking more sick leave or committing fraud as the person tries to find a way to fix the inequity. As a leader, you play a key role in ensuring that the amount your team members are paid is fairly distributed.

STEP TWO: Motivate with progress

Another key motivational lever is progress. To be motivated, people in organisations need to be able to get things done. If you're a leader, sometimes this means you need to get out of the way and let your team just get on with it. This doesn't mean you leave them rudderless or without direction. Set the direction and help your team know the desired outcome, but empower them to have the courage to move forward and give them the skills to be able to do that in their own way.

A very useful 2010 study from Harvard found that one of the biggest demotivators for people in the workplace was a lack of progress.[45] The research asked the leaders and the workers the same question to uncover what motivated employees. There were five options put forward:

- Recognition for good work

- Incentive and rewards
- Sense of progress
- Clear goals and targets
- Inter-personal connections.

When the managers were asked what they thought the answer was, they selected 'Recognition for good work'. But, for the employees who participated in the study it was a 'Sense of progress'. The researchers found that when workers thought they were making headway in their jobs, or when they received support that helped them overcome obstacles, their emotions were the most positive and their drive to succeed was at its peak.

In contrast, on the days when they encountered roadblocks their mood and motivation levels were at their lowest. The lessons coming out of this research is that it is incredibly demotivating for employees when leaders change goals autocratically, are indecisive, hold up resources and impede progress. This of course plays into the way our brain is wired. Our brain is more attuned to negative events than positive. It's not surprising that setbacks and delays, therefore, have a greater effect on people's emotions, perceptions and motivation levels.

This is why it is so important to make progress visible and to celebrate when you have made progress. Employees need to see they are heading somewhere and that their contribution is making a difference.

The story goes that before the first human landed on the moon a person visiting NASA was speaking to a cleaner and asked him what his job was. His answer: "I'm helping to put a man on the moon". This person, in a role that many people would see as non-core to getting a man on the moon, didn't see it like that. He could see the bigger picture. Despite his role being a non-technical role he could see the part he played in helping the organisation achieve its goal. Imagine in your organisation if you were able to achieve such clarity of vision and purpose for every employee.

Progress does not come without skill and capability. It's essential to have the right people in the right jobs doing the right things. Everyone is good at 'something', and that 'something' is different for every member of your team. It's important to know what that 'something' is and to understand whether those skills are being utilised in their current role. Are they at capacity or is there stretch? This stretch is important because typically people who are not stretched in their role become bored, complacent or both.

Mihaly Csikszentimahalyi devoted much of his life to examining this concept.[46] Originally his work started with artists. He was curious as to why it was that artists could get so immersed in their work that they could work for days without eating. He then transposed his work to the business environment. He found that people get into a 'flow' state when they are focused on a task for intrinsic reasons. In this state, there is the optimal mix of skill and challenge. I characterise it as feeling like you are in the zone, such that work becomes almost effortless.

Mihaly's research found that there were five conditions for flow:

- Clear and attainable goals
- Strong concentration on a focused topic
- Intrinsic motivation
- Balance of the challenge with your ability
- Immediate feedback.

In my work with teams from many different organisations and industries, I often ask them to reflect on a time they worked in a high-performing team. This team may be in a work, social or personal setting. What always comes up in these discussions is that they felt highly motivated; the team was achieving great things; they felt empowered and supported; and they loved what they were doing. Interestingly, in most cases they weren't working on something that was easy. Often the goal was incredibly challenging and they were working long hours. It didn't feel too hard because the right environmental conditions were in place for success.

Unfortunately, often some or all of these elements are missing in an organisational context. The good news is that as a leader you can change this. You can create the environment where your team feels the right level of challenge but also supported and equipped. This may include: crafting clearly defined goals, paying attention to how roles are structured, ensuring there is capability to carry out the work, providing regular feedback, as well as providing an optimal level of decision-making autonomy. The greater the ability for your team to be cohesive and secure progress, the better able you will be to influence.

STEP THREE: Motivate during change

Knowing the nature of people and how to motivate becomes even more important during periods of organisational change.

Surprisingly, often when organisational changes are made little thought is given to the impact this will have on employees. Instead, leaders try to ram changes through. They assume that everyone is OK. They don't take the time to listen to their team, and to find out what is going on for them and what support they need.

As a leader, a minor change in strategic direction may be irritating for you but what does it really mean for the work your employees are doing? Are you taking the time to find that out and to understand what support they need to work through it?

All change involves a period of transition and so it is inevitable that there will be a period where people feel unsettled and momentum is lost. None of this is to be unexpected. Once again, this comes down to how our brain is wired. The brain hates change that is externally imposed and so people resist change when it is forced upon them. People want to know what the change means for them and what they stand to gain or lose. They want to be involved and not left 'out of the loop'.

If you think back to the section on your mindset earlier in the book, you'll recall that people bring assumptions and expectations from their past experiences to the present situation. As a result, if the last change they experienced was horrible and challenging they will be sceptical about this one. This is exacerbated if trust is low in the team. They will be wary of the motivations for the change. If employees see or smell self-interest and hidden agendas from the leaders, trust evaporates, motivation drops, and productivity plummets.

Your brain is constantly making decisions – is this a good thing for me, or is it a bad thing? Is this situation a threat or is it a reward? Making a threat–reward decision is your amygdala at work, and it is part of human nature. It is this survival mechanism that kept humans safe back in ancient times. However, in those days the threat was a physical threat. Today, the threat may be a change in circumstance or a challenging interaction with someone.

Your brain treats these social and personal interactions as a threat or reward, with the same intensity as if it were a physical threat or reward.

David Rock's SCARF model is useful to understand at this time.[47] It is based on the framework that there are five domains of human social experience which activate either the primary reward or threat circuitry in the brain:

- **Status** – relative importance to others – pecking order, hierarchical authority and seniority
- **Certainty** – being able to predict and know what is going to happen

- **Autonomy** – sense of control over events and having choices
- **Relatedness** – sense of safety with others and concern for the group in which you are a part
- **Fairness** – perception of fair exchanges between people.

Each person has one of these elements as a primary activator. The best way to explain this is through examples. If status is your primary activator, your threat response will be activated if you are demoted at work, or someone does something to you that makes your status feel like it is under threat. If certainty is your primary activator you will be concerned about not knowing what is going to happen. While with relatedness if a colleague has something happen to them that concerns you, your activator will be on.

There are things you can do to minimise or exacerbate the impact of those triggers on yourself and others. This is discussed in the next section on page 158.

CREATE A NEW NARRATIVE

> "We have to start by changing the mental maps that have guided our actions in the past. We have to move from the individual out, rather than the organisation in."
>
> —*Professor Black, INSEAD*

Now that you have an understanding of how people are motivated, what do you do about it? Understanding people is one thing but it's useless if you don't translate it into action. It's like reading a recipe book and never cooking anything out of it. It's interesting but there's no outcome. If understanding people are the insights, then this section is about creating the new narrative. And this narrative is going to help guide your action so that you can put those insights into practice.

Much of this narrative will be considered in the context of change. Why? Because all organisations go through constant change. To be successful and influential you need to be able to secure successful outcomes. That is, get change embedded in the organisation's processes and people's behaviour, and ensure it sticks! Doing this involves interventions that are planned and acted on at the individual, team and organisational levels. A conscious change leader knows what needs to be done for each of these levels to build buy-in, and ultimately support and acceptance. In short, they practise conscious leadership and know how to get things done through other people – the ultimate test of influence.

As the ancient Chinese philosopher Lao-tzu said:

*"…learn from the people
plan with the people
begin with what they have
build on what they know
of the best leaders
when the task is accomplished
the people all remark
we have done it ourselves…"*

This is a beautiful reflection and it represents the basis for the type of relationships I am advocating.

STEP ONE: Lead consciously

There's no doubt that being a leader is daunting. Leaders today face a myriad of challenges because the problems they encounter are often not predictable. Innovation is coming from unlikely sources and non-traditional players in the market. There is often ambiguity about how and when to make decisions and the expectations on leaders are not diminishing. Combine this with conflicting priorities, hidden agendas and internal politics and it stacks up as a lot to deal with.

Stroll into a bookstore and you'll see shelves and shelves of books on leadership. There are thousands of books and many, many leadership models. At the core of most of these theories are the basic tenets of human decency and good manners: be a good person, treat people with respect and the way you want to be treated; be kind, humble and honest; have integrity; and show compassion. If you think about it, none of these concepts are revolutionary or groundbreaking. They're elements that all of us can grasp.

I'm not going to provide an outline of different leadership theories but you may want to take the time to read Bill George's *True North*. Out of all the leadership books I've read it's one that's really resonated with me. He outlines five characteristics of effective leadership:

- Pursuing purpose with passion (understand yourself and your passions and how to get a sense of purpose)
- Practising solid values (which are best tested under pressure)
- Leading with heart (making tough choices with compassion empathy and courage)
- Establishing enduring relationships (that are long-lasting and open)
- Demonstrating self-discipline (to produce results).

He also provides some really useful exercises to help you work through whether your values and the work you do are aligned.

If you are to lead consciously, you must understand your leadership style.

Consider this scenario: you've been asked to lead a transformation in your workplace. What's one of the first steps that you take?

Is it to sit back and identify how your team members or colleagues need to change? Or do you think about how you may need to change?

For most people, myself included, it's easy to recognise what you think needs to change in other people, but it's much harder to identify it in yourself. And yet, if you are consciously leading change you need to be prepared to change yourself – your mindset, operating style, management mode and leadership behaviour.

Robert Kegan and Lisa Lahey, who have studied why many crucial change efforts fail, found that one of the core problems is the gap between what is required and a leader's own level of development. As they state in their book, *How the way we talk can change the way we work:* "…*it may be nearly impossible for us to bring about any important change in a system or organisation without changing ourselves (at least somewhat)*…".[48]

Understanding what personal changes you may need to make through the change process goes beyond pinpointing new technical skills. It's about delving into the meaning that drives your behaviour and finding the mental model you are applying to the decisions you are making and actions you are taking.

This requires you to be conscious of your leadership style and observable actions. To do this, start thinking about your 'leadership moments of truth'. That is, those actions that you take (often subconsciously) which define how your leadership style is viewed by colleagues, peers and team members.

✅ CHECKPOINT ACTIVITY

When thinking about an interaction or a decision you've made recently, ask yourself:

- ☐ What was going on for me at that moment?
- ☐ How might that decision be perceived by others?

- [ ] Were my words and actions inconsistent in any way?
- [ ] Was I playing favourites with people in the team?
- [ ] Was I living up to my commitments?
- [ ] Were my behaviours authentic and values-driven?
- [ ] What was I paying attention to and prioritising?
- [ ] If something went wrong, how did I react?
- [ ] How have I been allocating resources and rewards?
- [ ] How have I been recruiting and promoting people in the team?
- [ ] Was I leading with my head or my heart?

Truthfully answering those questions will help you start to identify the triggers for your behaviour. Those triggers may be situational or people-related. Knowing what triggers an unhealthy or unhelpful behaviour is the first step in addressing and ultimately replacing it with something better. This isn't an easy thing to do and you may want to get advice and input from a trusted colleague because we can be blind to our own behaviour. Don't be afraid to ask for support. A trusted friend or adviser, a mentor or business coach may be very supportive in helping you reflect on your behaviour and to create the necessary insight that is a precursor to personal change.

> **STEP UP TIP**
>
> The more open you are to the feedback that is offered, the more valuable you will find this exercise. Feedback can be hard to hear. I'd encourage you to not immediately discard the pieces you disagree with. While not all the feedback will be correct, or perhaps helpful, there is usually a grain of truth in the feedback. Take the time to find the grain and determine what it is really telling you. Significantly, listening to feedback can provide an opportunity for a whole new relationship with someone.

I always recall an episode with a colleague of mine many years ago. We were in a team session and we had to individually talk to each person and tell them something we would like them to stop doing, start doing and continue. When this team member got to me it felt like she 'ripped into me'. Comments such as: "You judge me", and "I feel like you're always looking over my shoulder and checking on me". It went on for quite a while and it felt really brutal and unfair. My immediate reaction was to want to argue back, but I held it in. I spent the next 24 hours ruminating over the comments. I realised that we had very different perspectives on why I was acting how I acted. We needed to talk further.

The next day I invited her to have lunch with me and she accepted. Over lunch I explained that I really valued her work and thought that I could learn from her and that was why I asked lots of questions. My interest in her work was not about judging but about my own learning. She was surprised and flattered. We talked for quite a while about our different perspectives. Ultimately, we went on to build a really fantastic working relationship and friendship. I learned a very powerful lesson that day: people can easily misinterpret your actions and that can lead to serious misunderstandings and unnecessary conflict.

Leading when times are good is easy. At the start of a project, you can get swept up in the initial enthusiasm for it and be overly optimistic about delivery timelines and benefit schedules. But, as the work progresses, challenges will inevitably be encountered. Obstacles and roadblocks that weren't expected will arise, making progress slower and more difficult than planned. What looked easy in the beginning, seems much harder in the middle.

It's challenging when things go wrong. You may start to feel anxious and uncertain, particularly if you see momentum waning and milestones slipping. When the team starts to question its ability to deliver, and teamwork starts to suffer your leadership is more critical than ever. As a conscious change leader you need the courage and fortitude to work through difficult times.

This requires leadership – where you are leading with your head and your heart. The most wonderful aspect, however is that the more you adopt this leadership style, the more engaged your team will be. They'll know that you have their backs. They'll recognise that you support their efforts to try new things and to make progress. Your actions will show them that you realise you can't make progress alone. It will also show that you value their efforts to push themselves and to explore, create and refine until the desired outcome is realised.

STEP TWO: Lead individually

Change happens one person at a time. In organisations this can be forgotten. Change is often considered at an organisational or team level, ignoring the fact that it's each impacted individual that is required to change. Every person has a different comfort level for change. When you are leading people you need to think about each person in your team as an individual. This can be hard, particularly if you have a big team with multiple layers of management. In that situation, you have to rely on others to help – particularly your direct reports (i.e. the people who report to you). They play a key role in supporting and encouraging the people who report to them.

Ask yourself: do you believe that people can change and improve? This is an important question to answer. Because if you have a fixed view on a person's characteristics and their ability to learn and grow, that mindset will come through in how you talk to them and how you treat them.

You need to trust them, and they need to trust you as well. To gain a person's trust, first take the time to get to know and understand them. This goes beyond understanding their skills, to understanding what motivates and drives them, as discussed in the earlier section, Nature of Motivation (see page 140). Understanding their neurologically based trigger points helps. Is the person driven by status, fairness, certainty, autonomy or relatedness?

Knowing, for example, that the individual's trigger point is status will help you better frame the message and so better communicate with them.

To do this, refer to Figure 16 and identify the trigger which is most activated in the person. Then ask yourself the questions and consider the suggested actions to take to best minimise the trigger's impact.

You may want to do this as an activity with your team. It's important to not assume that you have selected the right trigger for a person. What triggers them may be hard to know. You'll have more insight if you talk to them about this, and give them a chance to self identify in a safe environment.

From my experience working in and around change for more than 20 years I've found that change is so much easier the more that people are involved. People don't like change that is thrust upon them and when they feel like they have no say in how they are being treated. It's important to find ways for people to be involved and, while they may have no say over the end outcome, there may be ways they can be involved in the process.

When I was leading a team, I was given a fixed reduction target for the number of employees I needed to remove from the team. Now I couldn't change that number. What I could influence though was how I managed the process with my team. I decided to be upfront with my team and tell them what I needed to do and that I wanted their help in working through the solution. I was a little unsure as I hadn't tried this approach before. It turned out to be a fantastic approach. As we jointly worked through the new team

Figure 16: Discovering and minimising trigger points

Status	**Questions:** Will this change impact how team members view their level of capability and capacity? Does this change impact their hierarchical position? Does it impact their status in some way? **Actions:** Make people feel valued; provide genuine feedback; give people a reason to want to move from current to new state and explain what it will mean for them; get them involved and if possible, give them a say in how they get involved.
Certainty	**Questions:** Am I aware of the scope of the change? What's the impact and likely outcome, and can I share these details? Are there unresolved elements? How can I best provide certainty and clarity? **Actions:** Discuss rumours openly; be explicit about key messages; if you can't communicate the details, let the team know when details will be available; break the change into smaller, manageable steps – with clear goals; keep progress visible.
Autonomy	**Questions:** What's my level of control over the change (and my team's)? Will my team have involvement (design or delivery)? Will my team have a say over how the impacts play out, and how they are trained or supported? How much choice can I give people in the team? **Actions:** Involve people in the change and provide choice; provide channels for self-directed learning; avoid micro management; offer support; welcome feedback and ideas.
Relatedness	**Questions:** How connected are the people impacted by the change? Does the change negatively impact how the team will work together and interact? **Actions:** Humanise the message; establish common ground – be inclusive; look for opportunities for social connection and support; promote informal collaboration channels; set up buddy and mentoring systems; show the team they matter to you.
Fairness	**Questions:** Will the team perceive they are being treated fairly with respect to the change? Will there be concerns about favouritism? **Actions:** Be open and transparent about what is changing and why; ensure you treat everyone equally – don't play favourites; give everyone a chance to be involved – equally.

structure it became clearer what changes needed to be made. People were then happy to put their hand up and offer to leave as they could see that their role was not going to be needed in the future. No one felt pressured to leave and because people were involved in creating the options they were happier with the process and the outcome.

Supporting your team through change also involves making sure they have the skills and capability to change. This is a delicate balance of people feeling the right amount of focus and challenge, as well as being supported and equipped to change. There must be clear goals, an implementation approach, progress updates, immediate feedback and the appropriate level of engagement and support. People want to be involved with the change, so it's important to consider the impact on them, the degree of autonomy possible in how the change is implemented, as well as the capability uplift required to embed and sustain the change.

More and more evidence exists as to the importance of building new habits as part of the change process. We all have habits.

Habits shape what you do and therefore impact what you will or won't achieve each day. American writer and poet, Ralph Waldo Emerson, once said: *"Sow a thought, and you reap an action; sow an action, and you reap a habit; sow a habit, and you reap a character; sow a character, and you reap a destiny".* It's a great way to think about the massive impact that a subconscious habit can have on outcomes in your life.

What's common is that it is hard to change a habit. When you think about habits in the context of organisational change, it is not surprising that it is difficult to get organisations (and the individuals who work there) to change. This is because change isn't a linear process. It requires ongoing reflection, attention and action. It involves building new habits.

To thrive through change individuals need to understand their habits and know how to change them. Habits are built over time and they operate to save the brain effort. Your clever brain finds lots of ways to save energy. Creating habits is one such device.

Academic researchers, Bas Verplanken (University of Bath) and Wendy Wood (Duke University), found that more than 40% of the actions people performed each day weren't decisions, but habits.[49] This means there is an incredible amount of behaviour that is automatic and carried out almost unconsciously.

Habits can be changed but it takes effort. The interesting thing is that habits can be created subconsciously or consciously. Changing a habit and replacing it with a better or new habit needs to occur consciously. Verplanken and Wood also found that *"Successful habit change interventions involve disrupting the environmental factors that automatically cue habit performance"*. Significantly, the process used to change a habit isn't determined by whether that habit arises in a personal or work context.

Changing a habit involves 10 key steps. In this scenario, I've used a simple example of someone trying to stop eating too much chocolate.

1. Identify the habit you want to change. *For example, you'd like to stop eating too much chocolate.*
2. Acknowledge that the status quo can't remain and recognise and accept your part in changing it. This is about accepting the fact that it's your decision to eat chocolate and your decision to stop. Only you can make the change.
3. Uncover what is motivating the current behaviour. The chocolate fetish may arise when you are bored, or it may be triggered when you are stressed at work.
4. Identify ways of changing, including what you may need to disrupt in your environment to make the change

successful. This may involve changing the way you walk home so that you don't go past the corner store to buy chocolate or making sure there is no chocolate at home.
5. Start making changes in small steps, as it's often easier to break a habit when it is broken down into a series of smaller, more achievable activities. This could include a regime of not eating chocolate during the working week, but allowing a treat on weekends.
6. Commit to your changes publicly because it's much harder to renege when you've told other people you are going to do it. You could post the commitment on social media or tell someone who can help keep you honest.
7. Find a buddy who you can undertake this journey with, so you can support each other through the process.
8. Monitor how you are progressing and keep the results visible. Keep a track of the number of days you haven't eaten chocolate and post it on your fridge at home.
9. Celebrate your momentum by rewarding yourself as you've made progress. Of course this reward shouldn't involve more chocolate!
10. Keep moving forward despite setbacks. Inevitably the progress of habit change won't be perfect and you may find you slip back into old habits. Don't beat yourself up when you do. Acknowledge the slip, be kind to yourself and then get back to it!

Looking for ways to help your team and colleagues build new habits can be useful. This is because change – when it looks large – can appear daunting. However, if it is broken into more manageable pieces it looks easier to accomplish. It's like the saying: "How do you eat an elephant? One bite at a time".

It's not easy to get people to change if they don't want to change. If you want people to establish new habits and routines in the workplace, think about what you can to do to lead the way. Leadership and what you do, or don't do, is critical. Your team and colleagues will be watching.

STEP THREE: Lead collectively

I've worked with many teams over the years. What was common is that the best teams knew that a successful team environment was not just about the task that needed to be done but about how the task was done and how they worked together to accomplish it. They knew that the outcome would be better because of the team, and that they would more likely reach their goals if they worked collaboratively.

If you want to be a conscious change leader, it's your responsibility to create and nurture the right type of team environment. Doing this is essential if you want to be influential. Leaders who are influential know how to build great teams, and they know how to lead teams through different phases of their life cycle and through change. They also know how to best leverage the strength of each individual to collectively harness the power of the team.

If you want to see whether your organisation has a robust and healthy culture, look at how it handles disagreements and differences of opinion. People often think that having a healthy team environment and organisational culture means everyone needs to agree – all the time. It's the fallacy of 'consensus rules'.

The fact is too much consensus is unhealthy. When you have team members and colleagues unwilling to challenge or disagree with each other, you're setting the scene for future failure. People in organisations need to be able to robustly discuss and disagree as part of the decision-making process. ANU Professor, Andrew Hopkins, has written extensively on risk failures and the dangers of consensus decision-making.[50] As an expert in this field he's found that groups are often more inclined to make riskier decisions than individuals. This is because of the process of de-individualisation.

How this plays out is that because there are many people responsible for the decision, the individual feels as though they are not personally responsible for it. They are therefore more likely to take risks and can be persuaded by the group to go against their own values.

It's important to encourage healthy debate and questioning and to explore ideas from multiple angles. This involves nurturing a culture where differences of opinion are seen as a good thing – an opportunity to fully examine an issue. When issues are not raised, they are just driven underground where they'll bubble up later.

Think about encouraging your team and colleagues to engage in spirited conversations, rather than silent, shallow or stunted conversations that don't advance the decision-making process. These are not aggressive conversations where one person dominates. Spirited conversations create energy, spark new ideas, help people think more clearly about the position they hold and open the room to different perspectives. It's about sharing your thoughts in the spirit of achieving a better and more robust decision.

Influential and conscious leaders lead, support, listen, inform and engage. They ask lots of questions and are constantly looking out for, and considering the needs of their team (see Figure 17).

Knowing your team and colleagues and where they are coming from is essential. This is easily done. Just ask lots of questions. You can keep it casual and chat over coffee.

Figure 17: Building a conscious cycle of interaction

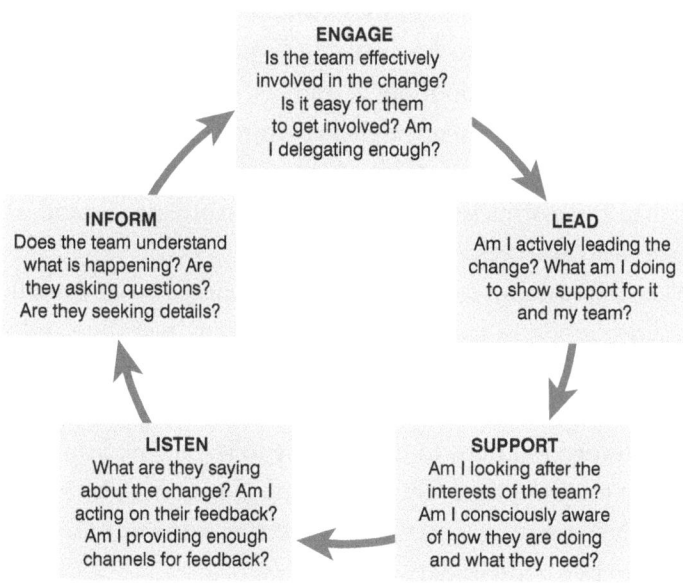

✅ CHECKPOINT ACTIVITY

Next time you are working on an organisational change ask your team members or colleagues:

- ☐ What do you like about the change?
- ☐ What's worrying you?
- ☐ What roadblocks or challenges do you think could make it hard for this change to succeed?
- ☐ How do you think these challenges could be overcome?
- ☐ What are the first steps you would take to do that?
- ☐ What do you think and feel would be a good outcome from this change for you, the team and organisation?
- ☐ What support would you find helpful?
- ☐ What do you need from me (your team leader) or others?

Answers to these questions will help you tailor your interactions and support in a way that is most useful and relevant to the situation.

To lead you need to be available to people – your team and colleagues. Keep your door open. And yes, this is still relevant even if you are working in an open plan environment with no doors. Be ready and willing to talk. Give people around you permission to challenge and ask questions. Find ways to involve people and listen to their ideas and concerns.

Most importantly, constantly communicate. Good conversations take time. Similarly, trust is only ever built up over time and it is only constructed if people know each other, respect each other and spend time together.

As a leader you need to devote time to leading and this means you need to spend time with your team. If you are spending your whole day in meetings and never interacting with your team it will be hard to be a good leader.

I was guilty of this when I worked for large corporates. I could easily get sucked into meetings that ran all day, never see my team and therefore only communicate late at night, and via email. It wasn't good. My team hated it. They hated the fact that they'd get emails late at night from me and hardly saw me – except when I was rushing from one meeting to another. I knew that if I wanted to be a better leader I had to find a better way. The only way to do that was to re-prioritise how I spent my day, and to make leading a top priority.

From my experience, the best leaders set aside dedicated time each week to spend with their team. They phoned their team members, rather than always emailing them. They had face-to-face meetings and made sure they knew each member of the team on an individual level. They also regularly scheduled team-building activities where the team could spend time getting to know each other and build connections.

The more effective your team, the more effective you will be, and ultimately the more influence you will have.

NURTURE RELATIONSHIPS

> "It is the individual who is not interested in his fellow men, who has the greatest difficulties in life and provides the greatest injury to others. It is from such individuals that all human failures spring."
>
> —*Alfred Adler, Austrian Psychotherapist*

Having healthy, thriving relationships is a cornerstone of a happy and fulfilled life. If you think back to the section on happiness (Practice 3: Upskill your set-point for happiness on page 47), one of the indicators of happiness was the level of connections that people have. Connections are critical if you want to influence outcomes in an organisation.

Relationships take on different forms. They can be: transactional, debt-laden or balanced.

Transactional relationships can be either once-off, irregular or frequent. They're not distinguished by the frequency of the interaction. They're distinguished by the nature of the interaction. In a transactional relationship it is clear that the interaction is just about the task at hand. It may be buying a cup of coffee or talking to someone at the bank. In both these examples you're the customer and there is a service that the other person is fulfilling. However, these types of interactions can be so much more.

Have you ever noticed how much better a transactional relationship is when you take it up a notch and make the effort to truly interact? That is, when you take a genuine interest in the other person, smile and ask them about their day. The relationship may still be temporary, but the characteristics and feeling that you have about the interaction will have changed. You'll feel better and so will the other person.

Debt-laden relationships are one-sided relationships where it is either all about you, or all about the other person. These relationships are hard going. You can feel incredibly bogged down if you are on the wrong side of it. Of course, for the person who is doing all the 'getting' it may feel good but only temporarily. These relationships are not sustainable. Eventually, one party will walk away.

Balanced relationships are where both parties to the interaction are looking to give and to gain. These relationships can be short or long term. They are characterised by a mutual understanding that both parties have something to offer and there is some connection or shared objective. It is from these interactions that a healthy and functioning relationship develops. Such relationships take effort and energy, but they are well worth it.

Relationships are critical in an organisational context. Often people feel the relationships they have in an organisation should be different to those they cultivate in their personal life.

I remember when I first started working, I had this strange notion that I shouldn't be 'friends' with anyone I worked with. I thought I should maintain a professional distance. This was particularly the case with team members. This was rubbish. I have no idea where I got this notion from, but I suspect it was something I observed during my formative years. I quickly learned that having friends at work made the workplace so much more enjoyable. With my team members I was much more able to build trust, loyalty and respect if I knew them and they knew me on a personal level.

Research supports this too. Tom Rath in his book *Vital Friends* refers to Gallup workplace research which found that having at least three close friends at work meant you were 96% more likely to be extremely satisfied with your life. Added to that, if you had a close relationship with your manager you were more than 2.4 times more likely to be satisfied with your job.[51]

STEP ONE: Build the foundation

There have been countless books written on how to build good relationships – starting with the seminal book by Dale Carnegie *How to Win Friends and Influence People*. All of these books outline the types of things you need to do to build strong and lasting relationships. The wonderful thing is that none of these elements are beyond anyone's capability. I always say "It's not rocket science", and yet we often find it hard to do. That's because we are human and no one is perfect. The important thing is to be conscious and aware when you interact with people. Try your best and, if you stuff something up have the courage to be vulnerable, admit the mistake and apologise. It's amazing how relationships can grow from vulnerability and authenticity.

Carnegie's rules, written more than 75 years ago, still hold weight today.[52] His advice was in many respects just basic manners. Things such as smile, be a good listener, remember their name and begin in a friendly way. He understood the importance of making the other person feel good about themselves, of showing respect and being genuinely interested in the other person. He also believed in the need to take the long-term view with relationships.

Tom Spaulding in his book, *It's Not Just Who You Know* adds to the Carnegie manifesto. One of the laws that he espouses, that really resonated with me, is the law of elevation.[53] This law is based on the notion that we make the most out of relationships when we are intentionally lifting others to places they can't go alone. This is a selfless way to build relationships. There are three primary elements:

- **Advancement** – helping people reach their full potential even when it has nothing to do with your skill or ability.
- **Link** – providing personal links to contacts and reaching out and extending your connections to people. This is not just about making email connections but going out of your way to facilitate connections across your network.
- **Lift** – honouring the person in some way either publicly or privately.

I love these ideas because they take the idea of relationship-building to a whole new level. Today, the frenetic pace and the advent of social media means we are connected, but often distracted. The connections can feel shallow and less personal. To stand out from the crowd you need to resort to some old-fashioned ideas. At the heart of this is the fundamental premise that you will find in every book about relationships – be authentically interested in other people. Unfortunately, in today's celebrity obsessed and 'me' generation some of this is getting lost. If you want to be influential in an organisation don't forget this. Instead, embrace it.

One of my managers early in my career had a remarkable ability to build great relationships and to get people to do things for her. If she needed to see someone and ask them to do something she'd drop around to their desk with a muffin. It was amazing what people would do for her because of the 'gift'. And she always remembered to say thank you. She was playing out Robert Cialdini's rule of reciprocity. He advocated that humans naturally felt obligated to do things for people when someone had done something for them. He saw it as pervasive and that *"By virtue of the reciprocity rule…we are obligated to the future repayment of favours, gifts, invitations and the like".*[54]

Over the years I've found that to build long-lasting and constructive relationships there are some fundamental elements to have in place, namely:

- Take the long-term view – this means that you give people the benefit of the doubt and assume good intent. You also never assume you know where a relationship may lead and so be open-minded and open-hearted with interactions.
- Be proactive in your interactions and patient. This means you are willing to extend the hand of friendship to people and are always looking for ways to strengthen the relationship. At the same time, you don't 'take' before you are willing to 'give'. Don't always think about what people can do for you, but what you can do for them.
- Pay it forward and extend support to people who may never be in a position to give you something in return. Just as others have helped you, so too you can pay it forward by helping others with no expectation of reciprocal gain.
- Build relationships intentionally – respect people's time and behave honourably. Find ways to maintain the connections – be it through regular catch-ups, thank you notes or offering to help them in some way.
- Find ways to involve people and get their advice. The focus is on their advice, not what they can do for you. People love giving advice and everyone wants to feel valued. Also be curious about the other person and what they have to offer. Ask lots of questions and remember that everyone has talents and ideas to share.
- Hold your ground, when necessary – and remember that a relationship built on trust will withstand consciously challenging conversations. Know how to say 'no' when it is needed but in a way that is respectful of the other person.

- Be yourself – share the real you with other people. Trying to be someone else will come off as inauthentic. It also uses way too much energy when you are trying to be something that you are not.
- Show gratitude and be generous – be thankful for what people are sharing and offering you. Wish your friends and acquaintances well and be genuinely happy when things go well for them. Gratitude is more than just being thankful for what is done for you. It is about being grateful for what you have and what others have as well.
- Genuinely wish everyone well. When you meet people and greet them, take a few seconds in your mind to silently wish them well. While this is a Buddhism practice which works to encourage people to spread joy and happiness to all, it is also a practice that promotes internal happiness.
- Know when to give up and move on. This is hard to do but unfortunately some relationships cannot be saved. This is particularly the case if the relationship is destructive or damaging to you in some way.

STEP TWO: Construct your network

Getting traction and gaining influence in an organisation isn't easy. Making progress on this front requires you to be able to build and leverage a strong network of stakeholders. It helps if you are deliberate about how you do this. Some people find this concept challenging and feel that it is 'Machiavellian'. It's not. It's just about being smart about how you construct your network. To be successful you need a network which is:

- **Broad** – includes a range of stakeholders both internal and external to the organisation, and across a range of functions.

- **Deep** – includes stakeholders at all levels in the hierarchy.
- **Established** – is based on trust, authenticity, reciprocity and transparency.

Building a network takes time and energy and it must be genuine.

☑ CHECKPOINT ACTIVITY

Ask yourself the following questions:
- ☐ Do you know how effective your network is?
- ☐ Does it help or hinder your ability to lead and make progress?
- ☐ Do you know how your stakeholders' rate their relationship with you? For each stakeholder think about how they would answer the following questions (inserting your name at the appropriate point):
  - ☐ Does *(insert name)* stick to their word? Are they trustworthy?
  - ☐ Does *(insert name)* care about this relationship?
  - ☐ Is *(insert name)* living up to the organisation's values?
  - ☐ Is the relationship with *(insert name)* worth pursuing?
  - ☐ Does *(insert name)* bring value and substance to the table?
  - ☐ Does knowing *(insert name)* help me in some way?

Be honest with yourself. Of course, your perspective may not be accurate, but at least you've taken the time to try and think about it from another person's point of view. If you don't know the answers to these questions, and you've never done a stocktake on the current state of your relationships you should. It's essential to understand whether you have bad, good or indifferent relationships with people in your network.

Additionally, think about whether you are doing a stocktake on the right people. While this sounds like a basic idea, it is easy to overlook when you are in the midst of the busyness of your work day – with lots of demands on your time. The solution is to take a structured approach to stakeholder management. The best way to do this is to use network analysis to interrogate your network and identify gaps and areas of focus.

The first step is to make a list of your stakeholders and identify if all the necessary relationships are in place. Once you've found gaps, consider what you can do to build a relationship with those people. You may discover there are people already in your network who have a strong relationship with them. If so, ask them to make an introduction. Be clear about why you want to meet the person and don't waste their time. Ideally, start this relationship-building process early. It is much easier to ask for something when the relationship is already well established. Get to know each person on a personal level – find out about their family, background, interests, etc. This will help you understand what motivates them and their agenda. Also, seek to understand who is in their network and who influences them. This provides useful insights into the other person.

You can think of your network as a spider's web. You are connected to people. They are connected to people – some of whom you know, and some you don't. Some of these connections are easy to see and others will be harder to see. Take time to identify the influencers in your network. These are typically people who other people want to know. They may be connected with people in positions of authority or they may hold some form of positional authority themselves. Also, look for the amplifiers in your network. These are the people who can get things done and can share information quickly. These connectors are important as they can help you navigate the organisation's complexity and also help you work around the bureaucracy (i.e. get things done through the 'back door').

As you do this exercise, you will start to build a picture of your network. This may look a little messy but it will be really helpful to see how people are connected. You'll also be able to clearly identify where there are gaps in your network.

> **STEP UP TIP**
> Don't fall into the trap of thinking that the influencers and amplifiers are always going to be in more senior positions. Some of the most powerful people in organisations are the Executive Assistants. They're the gatekeepers to the executive's diary and it pays dividends to have really good relationships with them. They'll get you in the diary and they can get you taken out!

Once you have outlined your map of networked stakeholders – known and unknown – start to look at their characteristics in the context of the work you are doing. For each stakeholder do an 'as is' and 'to be' assessment. That is, where is the relationship now, and where does it need to be. This involves:

- **Assessing the health of the relationship** – is it healthy or unhealthy?
- **Looking at how frequently you interact with each other** – is it frequent, infrequent or sporadic?
- **Understanding their position in the organisational hierarchy** – are they a peer, team member or more senior than you?
- **Identifying where there are relationship gaps** – are there key people who you need a relationship with who are missing in your network?
- **Pinpointing the key relationships** – who are the key relationships, influencers and amplifiers in your network?

If you are leading a change program you would also want to know the following about each stakeholder:

- **The role they are playing with respect to the change:** Stakeholders typically take on one of these roles: they are either involved in making the change happen, watching it happen or trying to stop it happening. If they are actively supporting the change they will be working to make the change happen by backing decisions, providing resources and offering input. Alternatively, they may be happy to support the change if they are enlisted to provide assistance. On the other hand, they may be ambivalent about the change, so they are not actively engaged in the change and are on the sidelines watching it happen. Lastly, they may be working against the change and trying to stop it. Having a clear picture of the role each stakeholder is playing helps you understand what type of engagement you need to have with them and how or when you should be getting them involved with the initiative.

- **Their ability to influence the change:** What position does the stakeholder have in the organisation? Are they a decision-maker who provides the 'go/no-go' decision on the change? Are they are a recommender, where they hold a position of influence with a decision-maker so they can advise whether a change should be stopped, started or continued? Lastly, do they have little or no impact on the decision? Understanding the influence they have helps you prioritise how much time you should be spending with each stakeholder. The higher the degree of influence, the more time you will need to devote to them.

- **The personal impact the change will have on them:** This is important as the stance a stakeholder takes on a change initiative may be influenced by the personal impact the change has on them. Will the change impact their role, level of position/authority in the organisation, and their perceived ability to be successful in the organisation? While individuals might say their decisions and actions are not influenced by personal impact, despite their best intentions, their judgment may still be clouded. Understanding the nature and extent of the impact means you can be conscious of it and factor it in to your engagement strategy.

Looking at all these elements helps to paint a picture of the issues and concerns of your stakeholders and their ability to impact the success of the change initiative. For example, if a stakeholder is actively working against the change, is a decision-maker, and the change is likely to impact them personally you'll have to work hard to get them onside. Think about the supporters who can counterbalance the influence this person may have on decisions and outcomes.

In contrast, if there's a stakeholder actively working against the change and they have no ability to impact decisions then they are less likely to be able to derail the initiative. In this case, you won't need to spend as much time getting them involved and on board.

 STEP UP TIP
Always take a long-term view as stakeholders can change quickly in organisations and someone whom you may currently view as not relevant can quickly become a critical stakeholder.

STEP THREE: Nourish your network

Once you have built your network map, and understand your stakeholders you'll be able to build a plan to address where there are deficiencies and also take action to maintain and continue to enhance the already healthy relationships. You'll also be able to think more strategically about the approach you are taking to building your network and what you can do to expand your base from its current position. This involves considering how you can use your existing relationships as points of connection and leverage to broaden and strengthen your network. This is particularly useful when you are trying to build a coalition of support for an idea.

The approach you adopt can look something like Figure 18, where you take a structured and planned approach to building a support base for your idea or initiative.

Figure 18: Building a stakeholder base to secure support

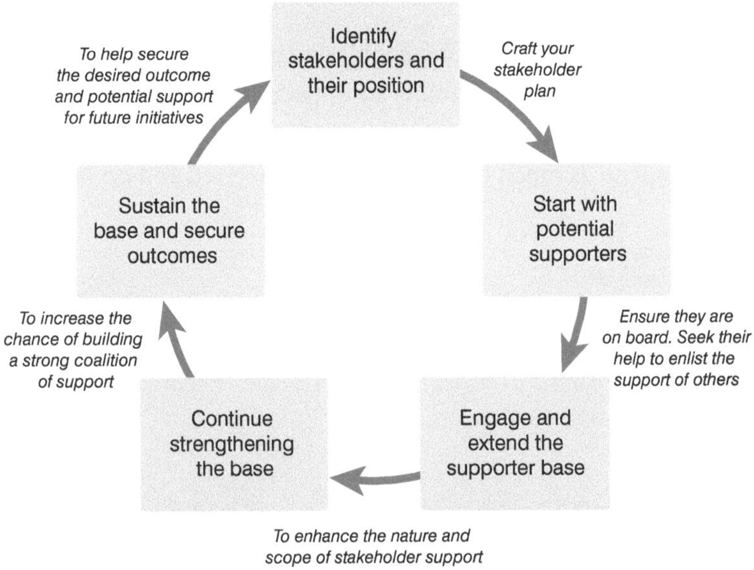

Setting aside dedicated time each month or each quarter to review and discuss your stakeholders is essential. This can be done individually or as a team. For example, in a large-scale transformation program I worked on we devoted half a day each quarter to running a detailed stakeholder planning session. Prior to this session we would review our stakeholder lists for currency and to ensure our understanding of issues and concerns was up to date. At the session, we would debate the stakeholder's position regarding the change and what actions needed to be taken in the next quarter to harness support. We would also review actions from the previous quarter.

The session's power was in the conversation which highlighted the different perspectives we had on stakeholders and their support or otherwise for the change. The conversations were robust and led to a much more focused, consistent and planned approach to managing stakeholders. If you know your hot spots and your areas of strength you will be in a much better position to build and maintain a strong coalition of support.

☑ CHECKPOINT ACTIVITY

Set aside some time to craft your stakeholder plan. Use the following ten principles to guide its development:

- ☐ Identify and assess your network. Ask yourself – who's in it, and how effective it is? Identify any gaps that exist, and where there are blockages (i.e. people with whom it's hard to get things done).
- ☐ Drive energy into your network. Strike the right balance between reaching out to people and asking for something, and you reaching out to others and offering help and support. Be proactive in helping others. Remember – the more you share, the more you will gain, over time.
- ☐ Consistently follow through and live up to your commitments. This is a critical ingredient for building trusted relationships.

- [ ] Consciously seek out people with different opinions who will challenge your thinking and mindset, and give your network diversity and depth. The more you broaden your mind the greater your ability to think issues through, take on different perspectives and manage complex change.
- [ ] Support your team and colleagues with their networks and understand how effectively they are collaborating. Is it effective? Are they collaborating across the team and into other areas of the organisation? How they network can impact your ability to influence.
- [ ] Know the amplifiers and influencers in your team and network. These people know people and therefore know how and who to influence. Simply, they know how to get things done and can more easily navigate hierarchical roadblocks.
- [ ] Reward and encourage people who engage in healthy and effective collaborative behaviours.
- [ ] Help integrate people who are new to your organisation and team. Introduce them to key people and let them know who they can turn to for information, expertise and support.
- [ ] Actively facilitate collaboration across teams, business units, and geographic boundaries, particularly where it's critical to business outcomes. You'll not only be helping to secure progress, but you'll also be building your brand as someone who is well connected.
- [ ] Enjoy building your network and always do it from a position of integrity. I've left the most important item until last. Your integrity is essential and it is something that you should protect and nurture. If you lose your integrity you will have little credibility or trust with your stakeholders, and therefore an ineffective network and an inability to influence.

Once you understand how to nurture relationships, the next step is to build your ability to have impact.

7. Craft impact

> "It is much easier to identify a minefield when you observe others wandering into it than when you are about to do so."
>
> —Daniel Kahneman, Psychologist and Author

In your lifetime you'll come across people who are charismatic. They often have an indescribable way of drawing people to them. They can be charming and disarming. Disappointingly, I often found that underneath the charisma there was a darker side. It was the case of all gleam but no soul.

This is a good thing to remember when it comes to impact, as unfortunately sometimes what impacts people is actually quite shallow.

Here's a really good example.

In the early 1970s, three psychologists from the University of Southern California ran an experiment where they invented a professor, who they called Dr Myron Fox. They hired an actor to play the role of the Professor. This actor fitted the image of what a Professor should look like. They also created a lecture that was fictitious. They then coached the actor on how to present the material. But, the material had a catch. There was no substance to the content and it was deliberately full of contradictory statements, double-talk and misleading comments.

But, he looked the part and he spoke with authority, clarity and confidence. It turned out that was all that mattered. The experiment was run three times. The first two times he delivered his speech in front of a room of mental health educators – psychiatrists, psychologists and psychiatric social workers. The third time to educators and administrators, the majority of whom were masters-level educated. In each of the experiments the feedback he received was highly positive.[55]

As Dan Gardner explains: *"As social animals we are exquisitely sensitive to status. An expert, in the appropriate circumstances, has considerable status. We respect that, even defer to it, whether consciously or not…"*[56]

How you talk. How you dress. What you say and what you don't say has a huge impact on how people perceive you. If you want to get traction in an organisation you need to have impact.

This can sound superficial. It's not. It's about being realistic about the world we live in and how it works. Having impact comes more easily to some people than others but everyone can acquire it – in varying degrees and forms. It just takes dedication and practice.

If you've been reading *Step Up* from the front cover to this point, you'll know that three of the four key elements required for influence – integrity, agility and insight – have been covered. The last element is impact, and it connects with each of those elements. It is very hard to have lasting impact in an organisation if you don't act with integrity. You may be successful in the short-term but eventually you will get found out. The same goes for agility. If you can't get things done and if you don't know how to produce results you will not have impact. And lastly, if you are unable to generate the people side of the equation to secure change you will not be successful. To gain influence in an organisation you need to have those three, plus the final element – impact.

Impact is about how you communicate and negotiate. Communication focuses on what you say, how you say it and when you say it. Negotiation is not just about securing agreement. It's about being able to match the strategy to the situation, secure alignment and build coalitions of support. When you can communicate with influence and negotiate wisely you have the confidence to create and sustain real value in an organisation (see Figure 19).

Figure 19: Creating value through impact

Widening the gap		Closing the gap
Misaligned	Integrity – staying true	Aligned
Unfocused	Agility – staying ahead	Focused
Traditionalist	Insight – creating change	Enterprising
Defeatist	Impact – creating value	Confident

COMMUNICATE WITH INFLUENCE

> "Live life as though everything is rigged in your favour."
>
> —*Rumi, poet*

Communication is a fundamental survival skill. You communicate constantly through your words, tone of voice, body language and other visual cues including how you dress. In fact, more than 50% of communication is non-verbal.

It's easy to create a list of the world's best orators. They command attention when they speak. They have presence. When you hear them speak you can have a visceral reaction because they know how to create an emotional connection that's deeper and more personal. For some of these people this skill is a gift they were born with. For many others it is a gift they have acquired through learning and practice (see Figure 20).

Figure 20: Components of compelling messaging

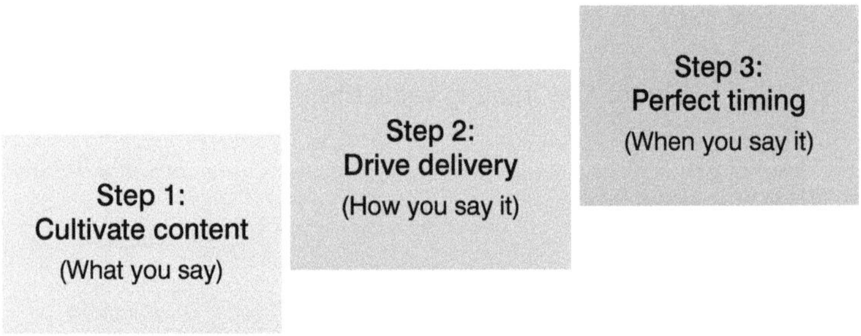

Step 1:
Cultivate content
(What you say)

Step 2:
Drive delivery
(How you say it)

Step 3:
Perfect timing
(When you say it)

Delivering a rational, credible and emotional connection

Regardless of the type of organisation you work for, being able to communicate persuasively is a real asset. There are some simple things you can do to elevate your communication to the next level – so that you are compelling and have impact in the right way and at the right time. All of this is about making connections with the people you are talking with; connections which are rational; emotional and credible in either a group or one-on-one setting.

Achieving this takes planning in terms of the content and practice in terms of how the message is delivered. You also need to consider the best time to deliver the message.

Unfortunately, when leaders communicate it's often unplanned and 'off the cuff'. Or at the opposite extreme, it's so scripted they appear inauthentic. It's a delicate balance to get the content, timing, tone and delivery of the message right. I'm not saying this is easy, but it's so critical it's worth investing the time and energy to master it.

When you communicate badly people around you end up:

- Receiving mixed messages
- Relying on the rumour mill for information
- Confused and not understanding what's happening and why
- Mistrusting you as you say one thing and do another
- Sceptical of your intent, with resulting impact on productivity, engagement and your ability to influence.

Learning to be a great communicator means you need to be open to feedback. I've worked with leaders who didn't listen. They assumed they were great communicators so didn't take the advice from people around them. They'd go 'off topic' and 'script' when they addressed staff at events and briefings. They'd use inappropriate language. They'd talk about themselves too much. In short, they hadn't bothered to understand the audience and what they wanted to hear. You'd see the staff tuning out to the message, and worse, their impression of this leader would be significantly diminished.

If you want to be more influential, take the time to learn, practise and listen.

STEP ONE: Cultivate the content

Content is critical. Content is about what you know, and what you then share with those around you.

The more you know the more confident you can be in sharing your opinion. Knowing more than others positions you to better shape outcomes and influence stakeholders. This is a delicate balance because you don't want to be a 'know it all' – the person with all the answers, all the time, who doesn't listen to other people's opinions.

You need to know your facts and be able to analyse them from multiple angles, while being receptive to other ideas (see Figure 21 below). The goal is to move from merely gathering content, to interpreting, listening and hypothesising. Each step up increases your confidence in sharing your ideas; in turn it builds your ability to influence.

Figure 21: Creating well reasoned and deliberate content

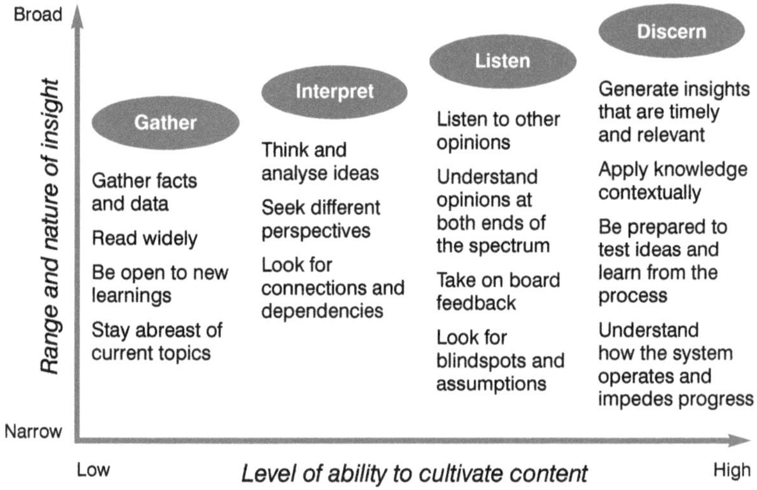

STEP UP TIP

Cultivated content is more easily developed if you read widely and stay abreast of current trends and world events. Earlier in the book I talked about the importance of learning. If you love learning you will have 'oodles' of content at your fingertips. Always be alert to what you can do to build your knowledge base of good content.

Forming a well-reasoned opinion means you take the time to analyse and interpret what you have read. This involves reviewing and reflecting on the information and crafting your opinion on what it means and why it may or may not matter.

Facts and analysis won't help you if you fail to listen. Failing to listen means you are not being alert to what else is going on around you. You'll miss the dissent and the voice of the minority, who frequently observe things that other people don't. Listening to them will help ensure that you are not captured by your assumptions, or blindsided by blind spots.

No doubt you've been taught the technique of active listening. While the process can feel a bit 'naff', the intent behind it isn't. There is nothing worse than talking with someone who is disinterested in what you have to say. They may be pretending to listen, but they're not really present and they're easily distracted. Worse still are those people who only hear part of the message – the bit that really interests them, or the part where they can add in their opinion or thoughts. At the other end of the spectrum are those people who are listening to understand. They are paying attention to what you are saying and not saying. They are listening with an open heart and mind.

To do this they are present, attentive and reflective. This means they are fully engaged in the conversation. Their focus is on you. They encourage and support the conversation. They know when to ask questions, probe further, remain silent and add commentary. They don't interrupt you. They are also attentive in terms of their eye contact. They face you, and with their body they lean in to the conversation. They are conscious of their hand gestures and the overall presence they are having. Lastly, they are reflective. This means they are able, when necessary, to summarise, clarify and reflect back on what you have said. They know how to match their tone of voice and pace with what is going on for you. They can comfortably play back the conversation to confirm understanding.

The art of listening in this manner provides benefits for both people involved in the exchange. The person speaking feels fully heard, while the person listening really gets to hear what is going on for the other person. The benefits on a relational level from this approach are enormous. It's a critical skill to master if you want to be more influential.

It is through this combination of gathering, interpreting and listening that you are able to hypothesise and create insights. This ensures you have worthy content to share with people; content which is well reasoned and deliberate. When your content is strong it is much easier to feel comfortable speaking up. Even when this means you are speaking against the status quo.

You may want to consider how you can use and share stories to support your content and bolster your point of view. Stories are typically constructed to include a beginning, middle and an end, along with context, an issue or conflict that needs to be fixed and a resolution.

Memorable stories will often come from your personal life. They can be very powerful connectors because people remember what they find personally interesting.

Story-telling is often thought of as a lost art. If you listen to great orators they will share defining moments in their life that shaped their future thoughts and deeds. Richard Branson is a fantastic story-teller. When you hear him speak he willingly and openly shares deeply personal events. He does the same in his books. He uses stories to share his business and life philosophies. He's also comfortable sharing stories where things haven't worked out. He knows the value in learning from mistakes.

Stories need to be real and while you can share stories about other people (i.e. people from history) it is much more powerful if the story comes from your experience. Stories help to build the belief of what is possible. They can be about where you've come from, experiences that you've had and what you've learned. But, be careful that the story doesn't overwhelm you or isn't appropriate for the audience. The story needs to suit the audience and situation.

> **STEP UP TIP**
>
> Don't make a story up. I worked with an executive who was delivering a speech to a large audience and he had worked with a speaking coach, who had helped him hone his message and delivery. He did a fantastic job and his speech came across really well. The only failure was that his introduction – which was a story – wasn't entirely true. While this wouldn't have been picked up by everyone in the audience, there were enough people from work at the event who knew the story was stretched to suit the purpose. It didn't look or feel good.

STEP TWO: Drive the delivery

Once you have your content, the next step is to think about how the content is delivered. Firstly, focusing on how you construct the words you use, that is, your message.

Abraham Lincoln is recognised as one of the world's best communicators. He understood the importance of knowing the audience and what they needed to hear. *"When I get ready to talk to people, I spend two-thirds of the time thinking what they want to hear and one-third thinking about what I want to say,"* he said.

Heeding that advice doesn't mean you shy away from the tough topics. It means you take the time to know your audience and understand their needs. Consider the audience and what will resonate with them. This includes being respectful and sensitive to their needs and circumstances, and using language they will understand and connect with.

Simple words and messages are often far more powerful. Lincoln's Gettysburg speech, which he delivered in 1863 to commemorate the Union soldiers killed at the battle of Gettysburg during the American Civil War, is recognised as one of the world's greatest speeches. He didn't use a lot of words to have an impact. Just 272 words in fact. Delivered in under three minutes.

If you can't explain what you are trying to say simply, your message is likely to get lost or go unheard. Don't over-complicate the message. Be approachable and accessible by:

- Not using technical words
- Dropping the jargon and not using acronyms
- Avoiding 'corporate' speak – i.e. words that are often meaningless
- Using language the audience will understand
- Matching your words to the situation.

Politicians are always taught to be 'on message' and you'll hear their 'sound bites' played over and over again in the media. These messages come across as staged and inauthentic. They seem contrived and rehearsed, and so most people don't connect with the message or the person delivering it.

So while I am advocating for simplicity, I'm also advocating for you to be direct, specific and authentic. Ground your messages in reality and what your team members and colleagues need to know. For example, if you are communicating about organisational change be descriptive. Paint the vision and describe what the future will look like in terms of how people will think, feel and act in the new world. Describe the benefits and be honest about the negatives associated with the change. People want to know: where and how they fit in; what they have to do and when; how they do it; what support they will receive; and how and when they can be involved.

Do all of this in a way that is 'real'. There is no harm in expressing emotion. Emotional language, used appropriately, shows that you care and have feelings. People will connect with the message better and, consequently, better connect with you.

Most of all, believe your own message. If you don't believe your own words, people will know. Why? Because your body language will give you away; unless you're an incredibly good liar.

Once you have the words constructed, consider the format of the interaction as that will help you prepare.

☑ CHECKPOINT ACTIVITY

Ask yourself:

- ☐ Will it be face-to-face, online, via an email or over the phone?
- ☐ Will it be one-on-one or in a group setting?
- ☐ If it's face-to-face, are you indoors or outdoors? Will the environment be noisy?
- ☐ If the conversation is private, will the venue be soundproof?
- ☐ Is the setting informal or formal? Will you (and those listening to you) be sitting or standing?
- ☐ Will any equipment you need be readily available?
- ☐ How much time will you have?

Remember, of course, that messages relating to and impacting people are always best delivered face-to-face.

If the session is face-to-face you'll want to pay attention to your style and presence. Part of this includes dressing appropriately. It may sound unimportant but making a positive impression has much to do with the image you project; and much of that is about what you wear. If you are delivering a message to workers in an industrial estate, dress for the site. This may include wearing the right safety equipment. It's about not over-dressing or under-dressing for the occasion. You need to project the right image.

Regardless of whether the medium is formal or informal, you should practise how you are going to deliver the message.

Delivery is crucial. Great speakers know how to use tone and pace to have maximum impact. They pause for effect. They speak slowly and clearly. They use intonation at the right moment to get attention, and they vary the pace of the delivery. They know how to use eye contact and gestures to draw the audience in. They also know what props to use to support the message – be that an image, poster, artefact or Powerpoint slide.

There's nothing worse than a message that is delivered at the same speed, tone and level. It's boring. You want to keep people interested so they listen, and then walk away with a clear understanding of what you were saying, why it's important, why they should care and what they need to do.

Most importantly, be friendly. If you smile, show genuine emotion and are interested in your audience, they will feel the warmth and authenticity of your message.

STEP THREE: Perfect your timing

Timing is critical in communication. It's about not being too early or too late with the message. It's about the right message, at the right time and in the right way.

Awareness is important. If you're wanting to have a 'tough' conversation, ideally wait until all those involved are in the best frame of mind to participate. Consider both the time of day and location. Make sure you aren't tired or agitated, as this will impact on how receptive you are to questions and challenging feedback. Maintaining composure and being empathetic is critical. You may also want to select a neutral or private location. The location is important as it sets the tone for the type of conversation you want to have.

Your communication needs to be rational, delivered credibly and have an emotional appeal that enables the listener to connect with it. This means you need to think before you speak and plan your timing, so that you know what to say, when to say it, and when to listen and be silent. Lack of preparation will show.

However, don't fall into the trap of delaying communication by waiting for the perfect time to communicate. Timing will never be perfect. Even if you don't have all the information, you can still communicate. People will respect you for your honesty. Be upfront about what you can and can't say. You may, for example, be able to provide a timeframe as to when you will know more and be able to share that information.

You are far better off communicating early and often. If you're dealing with an organisational change, for example, there's often a lot of information for employees to absorb and you need to regularly reinforce the messages using different communication channels. Importantly, be consistent with what you say and how you say it. This means you strive to ensure there's alignment between your words and actions. Your team and colleagues will quickly identify and assess any areas of disconnect.

Don't forget that communication is two way. It is not just about you 'talking at' someone. Instead, seek their input and listen to their ideas and perspective. Everyone wants to feel heard and you can create the space for this to happen. Welcome diversity of thought, knowing that it will lead to a better outcome.

Silence can also have an incredible impact. When you attend a meeting you don't always need to be the most talkative person in the room, or the one with the loudest opinion. I've worked with people who would spend a large part of the meeting watching the dynamics. They'd listen to what everyone would say and then very eloquently synthesise the opinions, pull them apart and put forward an alternate view for consideration. They'd play the role of the reasoned, dissenting voice. Delivered with reason and passion their message held sway, and they built a strong brand and ability to influence as a result.

NEGOTIATE WISELY

> **"Don't overlook small and seemingly insignificant negative actions. The smallest of sparks can burn down a mountain."**
>
> —*Tibetan saying*

While organisations may espouse corporate values this doesn't remove the fact that they are political-based systems. The reality is, therefore, that if you want to progress in an organisation you have to be able to navigate your way through the politics. That might sound harsh but unfortunately it's a fact.

Very early in my career, one of my managers said to me: "Michelle, you can get to manager level by being good at your job, but if you want to go higher you need to know how to play the system". At the time I thought the comment was wrong. I found out he was right.

On many occasions in my career I discovered that by holding my ground, backing myself and not letting someone push me into a corner I would come out in a far better position.

One particularly memorable situation: I had been working in an area that I really enjoyed and had a great relationship with my boss. She was tough, but fair, and I really admired her drive and intent. She moved to a new role and it was intimated that I'd need to consider finding a new role as the person coming in didn't work well with women. At the time, the comment didn't worry me as I had worked in lots of male-dominated environments and had always found a way to make it work. This time it was different. It very quickly became apparent that my new manager didn't value the work I did and had no interest in engaging with me. My team was surprised because the person was bypassing me and going direct to the males in my team with work. They didn't know what to do. This went on for a little while and it was clear that nothing I was doing was going to change his approach. So I needed to change mine. I've always found that tackling an issue head on leads to a better outcome.

At the end of one of our catch-ups, I said to him that from what I could see he didn't need me anymore as he didn't value the work I did or include me in things I normally managed. He appeared surprised. I responded by saying: "Clearly you're not ready for this conversation but I'm letting you know that I'm ready whenever you are". This gave me positional advantage. I had taken the first step.

A week later I got an email requesting I meet with him late in the day. My husband thought I'd get made redundant in the meeting; I, on the other hand, wasn't so sure. At the start of the meeting he pulled out an organisation chart. I could see my name wasn't in any of the positions reporting through to him. He talked for a while and explained his logic behind the new structure and how he was going to move my role to report to one of my current peers. Effectively, this would have demoted me in the hierarchy. My response was – "You've moved one-third of my role to this colleague, and another third to this person. That leaves one-third remaining, which you've repointed to report to this person. That's not a repoint. That's a redundancy conversation. You've just made me redundant".

The conversation went on for a little while and he didn't disagree with my comment about the redundancy. Towards the end of the conversation I asked what we did next and who I needed to talk to get the redundancy progressed. He said HR. This is when things got more interesting. It turns out he wasn't supposed to have made me redundant in that conversation; I was on a Talent Program and it never looks good when a person in the so-called 'Talent' population gets made redundant. This became very clear through my conversation with HR who kept talking about me being 'repointed' to a new manager. I was quite clear: "No. I've been made redundant". It went on for a while and eventually I said to the HR person: "It looks like you and my manager are on a different page. Perhaps, you should talk with each other and come back to me". She did and with the message that I wasn't supposed to have been made redundant, but because of how I managed the conversation he ended up making me redundant.

He completely underestimated me and my approach. That's positional advantage again. I knew I was good at my job and that I would easily find work elsewhere. I had good internal connections so I could find another job if I needed to. But, most importantly, I valued myself. I wasn't prepared to let a person treat me like that. I knew my rights and he had no right to demote me and make me report to someone else.

When I recounted this story to the people in my team they were surprised at my ability to negotiate and hold my position. One of them said to me: "Oh I would have just taken the role, even though I didn't want it". It became clear that some of my team felt they would have had no choice but to accept the changed role, given the difference in rank and power between them and the person in a more senior role. However, in this situation I took power by how I handled the conversation. From my perspective, I had nothing to lose and everything to gain. It's a great position to be in.

It made me reflect on how important it is to be able to negotiate. Technical ability will only get you so far in an organisation. To go further you need to be able to stand your ground and negotiate. It's a core survival skill. If you can't negotiate in an organisation you'll find it very difficult to get things done. And worse, some people will try and walk all over you.

The core elements in this book – mindset, integrity, agility, system and insight – culminate with impact's second ingredient, being able to negotiate wisely. If you have those elements in place you will negotiate from a much stronger position. If you know yourself and how you are likely to think, feel and react in circumstances it confers on you a mindset advantage over others. If you are well organised and prepared for your negotiation and agile you'll gain positional advantage. And lastly, if you have insight into how others think, feel and react and you can back yourself you'll have relational advantage.

It's time to negotiate with relationship, readiness and resolve (see Figure 22).

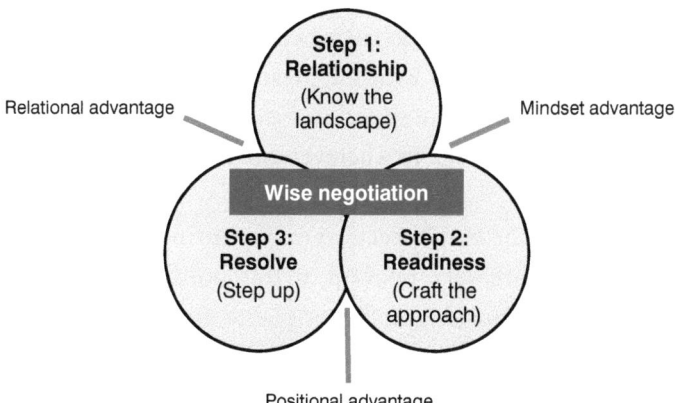

Figure 22: The wise negotiation approach

STEP ONE: Know the relationship landscape

Relationships are built on trust and understanding. You need to understand yourself – your character, capability and capacity. And you need to understand others in the same way.

Knowing yourself is an ongoing discovery. I don't think you ever stop finding out new things about yourself. Taking the time to know and understand yourself and what drives you is as important as exercise and eating well. It's like soul food. It nourishes you internally. And while it can be hard work, the outcomes make it worthwhile. As the ancient Chinese philosopher, Lao Tzu said: *"He who knows others is wise; he who knows himself is enlightened"*.

It is only once you know yourself that you can truly begin to like who you are and accept yourself with all your capabilities, faults and imperfections. If you don't like yourself it is very hard to have the self-belief and capacity to back yourself. If you don't back yourself, you'll never hold sway in a negotiation. You'll be like the leaf in the breeze, just floating around and at the mercy of whichever way the wind takes you. You deserve better. The more you are comfortable with who you are the easier it is to find your voice and to have the courage to use that voice wisely.

Using your voice and negotiating effectively is much easier if you have a good relationship with the person on the other side of the table. Of course, as in the situation I explained earlier, that is not always possible. However, to whatever extent you can, strive to build a relationship.

If you recall the earlier section on nurturing relationships, all those elements are very relevant at this point. The deeper and stronger the relationship, the better placed you will be. But, don't become complacent. Just because you have a relationship doesn't mean you'll get everything you want. It does however mean that you already have a foundation on which to build a conversation. This reinforces the importance of having broad and deep networks. Ideally, you want to have the relationship in place before you seek to leverage it.

If you don't have a relationship in place, consider what you can do to quickly build trust and rapport. There may be time before the meeting commences or in the weeks leading up to the negotiation. If possible, get to know some personal element of the other person's life. It might be their partner's name, or whether they have dog. Find some point of commonality on which the two of you can connect. The ability to make 'small-talk' when you meet is important. It sets the tone for the meeting and if done well it can be disarming.

Small-talk and other small gestures are critical. Be friendly. Be on time. Show appreciation. Treat them with respect. Be genuinely interested in what they have to say. Listen intently – always. Go out of your way to make them feel welcome. Be authentic and consistent in your interactions. People want people to like them, and so being likable will always work in your favour. If you show that you like them it's easier for them to like you. If they like you it's harder for them to take an unreasonable negotiating stance.

As I said earlier in the book, always take a long-term view with relationships because you never know where they will lead and when you may need to work with the person again. If you behave in a way that is unethical or out of line with your or their ethical position your integrity will be damaged and diminished in their eyes. Once damaged, it's almost impossible to recover.

During the negotiation continue to take a long-term view, and look for ways to build understanding and rapport. Ask lots of questions and discuss what matters to them. Be interested in their concerns and ideas. Be patient. Express your thoughts clearly and sincerely. Most importantly, mean what you say. A skilled negotiator will know when your words don't match your intent.

Your character is on display throughout the negotiation, as is their character. A negotiation is also a fabulous way of getting to know more about yourself and the other person. It is a learning opportunity. This fits very neatly with the concept of the growth mindset that was discussed earlier. Carol Dweck found that in negotiations those with a growth mindset were able to go beyond any initial failure by constructing a deal that *"addressed both parties' underlying interests. So, not only do those with a growth mindset gain more lucrative outcomes for themselves, but, more important, they also come up with more creative solutions that confer broader benefits".* [57]

STEP TWO: Be ready – craft the approach

Negotiations don't just have a beginning, middle and an end. They are far more circular than that, and often complex negotiations will have many rounds.

The first place to start is preparation. You don't want to walk into an important negotiation and 'wing it'. Well, you can try, but the outcome may not be good. This preparation is both physical and mental. You need to be physically prepared as negotiations can be tiring and draining. Make sure you are rested before any big conversation. You also need to be mentally prepared on two levels.

Firstly, be prepared for the mental challenges that happen during a negotiation. Your mind will be pushed and pulled in many directions. It's helpful if you go in to the situation expecting this to happen. Practise slowing your mind down so that it doesn't over-react to unexpected situations. This is where your mindfulness techniques can come to the fore. If you can maintain a calm demeanour and manage your internal feelings, your mind will be much more able to handle the discussion. If your pre-frontal cortex is overpowered by the 'fight or flight' situation, you will be less able to make reasoned and well thought through decisions. Part of this involves being emotionally detached from the outcome. This can be really hard to do, particularly if the issue really matters to you. However, the more attached you are to a predetermined outcome the far harder it will be to negotiate.

Secondly, you need to have your content prepared. This means you will want to know who you are dealing with and understand their style and approach. What do they want? What do they care about? A key part of this is understanding the subject matter in detail and the options that could be considered. Understand how your proposal could satisfy the needs of the other person, and be clear on your boundaries and priorities. Know what your non-negotiables are and what you are willing to give up. Having a clear trade-off helps you determine at what point you may need to walk away from the discussion. Also, think about what objections the other party is likely to make and how you will respond. It's helpful to know and analyse these options in advance – so you are prepared for all possible ideas and outcomes.

Your opening statement is crucial because often where the conversation will start is where it can finish. You need to know how to structure your argument for best delivery and receptiveness of the message.

> **STEP UP TIP**
>
> A simple trick is to practise delivering your opening comments, and focus on the key lines that you want the other party to understand. The more you practise delivering the message the easier it will become. You'll also become more confident. This is a key part of your preparation.

The more prepared you are, the more confident you can be. Confidence is crucial for the negotiation. If you aren't confident the other person will pick up on this very quickly. It becomes much easier for them to wear you down if they can see the 'chinks in the armour'. Always remember – it doesn't hurt to ask. Own your self-belief and the influence that comes with it.

William Ury, one of the authors of the bestselling book on

negotiation, *Getting to Yes,* and author of the bestseller, *The Power of a Positive No,* talks about getting to yes as a journey.[58] Along the way there are three yes's you need to secure from the other person:

- Yes to a wise agreement that addresses both parties' interests
- Yes to approval, so you can help the other party gain approval for the agreement from their stakeholders
- Yes to a healthy relationship despite the outcome of the agreement.

This is a really useful way to think about the scope of the process and the agreement. It helps to confirm that securing an agreement is about a relationship, and that both parties need to be clear on what securing an agreement means. This is about scope. It's also about having an understanding that a successful agreement is 'win-win', not 'win-lose'. Both parties need to walk away feeling comfortable and satisfied with the outcome.

It helps at the start of an agreement for each party to outline their perspective. By doing this you can understand, from both parties, the context, the issue and what's at stake. During this sharing of positions it becomes easier to see where there are points of commonality and difference. You can also start to build a common language. This is critical. Language can be a huge point of disagreement. I've seen many negotiations go off track because the two parties were saying the same thing but using different words. Common language builds connection and understanding.

As part of establishing the scope it's helpful to outline the process you'll be using to reach an agreement. The negotiation process and time taken will vary depending on the issue you are discussing. You will need to prepare for each step of the process. As one of my friends who is a highly trained negotiator said: "Success is 90% preparation".

While negotiations are not always a linear process, they will generally involve the following nine key activities:

1. Discussing and agreeing on the process for the discussion. Be warned: this can take a surprisingly long time.
2. Clarifying the issues that are being discussed so there is agreement on the scope and what is on the table for discussion. This too can be time-consuming.
3. Prioritising and working through each issue separately – often starting with the easiest issues first. It's easier to get agreement if you break the issue down into many parts. You can tackle each part individually and move on as you reach agreement on each point. That way there is clarity when an agreement has been made and it helps create a sense of progress.
4. Discussing the options for each issue. This involves considering the options from multiple perspectives and understanding the advantages and disadvantages for both parties.
5. Identifying the points of commonality and difference with respect to the issue, so there is a sense of where there is agreement and disagreement. You want to focus initially on the areas of commonality so that you can slowly move towards agreement. It's also about understanding what each person is willing to give up, and what are their non-negotiables.
6. Testing whether there is agreement on the best option to select.
7. If there's agreement – document the agreement and you can move forward to the next item.

8. If there's not agreement, keep discussing the options and the trade-offs involved until agreement is reach. This may involve modifying your offer, continuing to clarify the issue and their position and putting forward different options.
9. Once the issues have been resolved it's important to ensure this is documented and the steps for implementation are agreed before people leave the room. It helps if you take clear and detailed notes throughout the negotiation. Make sure you read back the written agreement to all parties – so the language reflects what has been agreed.

This process keeps going until all the issues have been discussed. Remember, negotiations can unfold in many different ways. Strategising how to best react and respond to those possible courses is a good use of your time. You need to be prepared for the unexpected.

As part of the preparation, think about the best time and location in which to hold the discussion. You may, for example, want to go to a location that is neutral. Getting out of the office – even to a cafe – can change the dynamics of the conversation. Avoid a set up that looks adversarial. The big boardroom table with you on one side and the other person opposite can be the wrong set up. If you are in a boardroom and there is one person you really need to get onside, if possible, make sure you sit next to them. As well, make sure you can have eye contact with them.

 STEP UP TIP
Don't try and negotiate when you're tired. Where possible, schedule complex and difficult negotiations in the morning when you're fresh and rested.

STEP THREE: Have resolve and step up

To negotiate wisely you need to have resolve. This involves being clear on the principles on which you will act, the perspectives you are taking into the negotiation and the effort or perspiration you are prepared to put in to the process to secure your desired outcome.

The more you are naturally curious about the other person's position and perspective, the more you will generate your own insights into what is going on for them. This is important. We all have assumptions and blind spots that can cloud our views. You may have a blind spot that is preventing you from seeing what is in front of you. Being open to understanding and learning will help the conversation progress.

What mental model are you applying to the discussion? Are you adopting a fixed or a growth mindset?

Are you thinking 'my gain'?

- I'm right – they're wrong
- I understand what's going on – they don't
- I'm being logical and rational – they're not.

Or are you thinking 'mutual gain'?

- I don't have all the answers
- I'm willing to shift my position
- I'm happy to test assumptions, share ideas and find common ground.

The stance you take matters. If you approach the negotiation thinking "It's all about me", you're more likely to end up with conflict, misunderstanding and poor outcomes. If you broaden your perspective and assume the good intent of others, you are more likely to have reduced conflict, heightened understanding and better outcomes.

Think about how you approach the negotiation – your thoughts, words and actions. It can help to have a set of principles to guide your behaviour. These principles become a reference point, particularly when things get messy and you feel the other party isn't playing fair. Your principles may include the following "I" statements:

- I believe that all good negotiations involve give and take. This is not about me winning 100% of everything all the time.
- I have the power to ask for what I want. I won't let the other person diminish my right to have a say.
- I can always walk away from a negotiation because for a negotiation to work everyone involved needs to negotiate in good faith.
- I won't criticise or demean the other person before, during or after the negotiation.
- I will always ensure the other person can finish the negotiation with their dignity intact.
- I will seek to build a constructive and long-term relationship with the other person. Where this isn't possible, I will maintain my dignity and integrity.
- I will always listen to the other person's point of view with my heart and my head.

Peter Block in his book *Flawless Consulting* outlines some ground rules for setting up a contract with a client.[59] These principles, with a few tweaks, are perfect ground rules to consider when you are embarking on a negotiation:

1. The relationship is 50–50, which means everyone has an equal responsibility in making the relationship work.
2. The negotiation should be freely entered into.

3. You can't get something for nothing – both people need to contribute.
4. All wants in a negotiation are legitimate.
5. You don't always get what you want, and you can say no to their want.
6. You can't force the other person to change how they feel or ask for something they don't have.
7. You can't offer what you can't deliver.
8. You can't make a deal with someone who is not in the room or a party to the agreement.

☑ CHECKPOINT ACTIVITY

Using the details on the previous page as a reference, take some time to write your negotiation principles. Share these with a trusted colleague to get feedback.

While having principles is a great starting point, they can be lost in the midst of a heated discussion. If you don't maintain your perspective throughout the negotiation you will be less likely to make wise comments and decisions. Having perspective means that you can be balanced and reasoned. This involves being prepared to listen with your heart and head. Techniques such as active and reflective-listening can be extremely valuable.

The other person needs to know that they have been heard. Give them space to put forward their perspective. Replay what you think they have said. Keep doing this until they affirm that you have understood their message. By hearing them, you demonstrate that you are genuinely interested in their perspective. This goes a long way to building empathy, rapport and trust.

Having perspective is also about having the skill to know what to say and what not to say, and what to share and what to hold back.

Timing is critical. There will be times for sharing, silence, listening and reflecting. Be comfortable to use all of these responses at times throughout the conversation.

Above all else, never publicly and openly criticise the other person. Separate the person from the issue. You can be unhappy with the issue and options, but you don't need to express your opposition in a way that the other person takes offence.

If I go back to the personal story at the beginning of this chapter, despite what was happening I always treated the person with respect. I was calm, polite and friendly. I never gave him cause to not like me or to want to 'get even with me'.

It is really useful if you can find ways to seek the other person's advice and, ultimately their cooperation. This can involve appealing to their ego and making them feel worthy and valued. People love to feel their ideas, and they themselves matter.

Your principles and perspective are irrelevant if you're not prepared to stay the course. Difficult conversations and negotiations can be tiring and taxing. They can wear you down. But, if the issue is important enough it's worth the effort. Consider what you need to do to make sure you are in the best possible state to engage in the conversation.

At the end of the day, what you put into it is what you will get out of it. If you want to be able to influence outcomes it's worth the effort!

8. What's next?

> "It is not because things are difficult that we do not dare; it is because we do not dare that things are difficult."
>
> —*Seneca, Roman Philosopher*

What's next? Well, that's up to you! If you want to *Step Up* and have more influence it's time to act. It's time to reflect on where you want to take your career and put these practices into action.

As I mentioned earlier, I'm inspired by the motto: "Feel the fear and do it anyway". It encourages action. I believe you have the power to make a difference to your life and the life of those around you.

If you want to gain greater traction and be more influential at work the only person who can make that happen is you.

The question is how much are you prepared to change to make this happen? How much does this matter to you? Clarity of purpose and resolve is critical if you are to step up.

I've never believed in a 'win at all costs' philosophy. If you understand yourself, work smart and hard, and stay true to your values you don't need to sell your soul to have influence. By understanding people, building strong relationships and being able to communicate and negotiate effectively you'll be able to better influence outcomes.

I'm hoping that your desire to influence is not a self-centred desire for power. Instead it's a desire to have influence so that you can effect good and healthy outcomes in your organisation. Outcomes that account for the needs of all stakeholders with a balanced, caring and compassionate view of the world.

Here's to your success in influencing for the good of all.

How to reach Michelle Gibbings

Learn more at:
www.michellegibbings.com
www.changemeridian.com.au

Follow Michelle on Twitter:
@michellegibbing

Connect with Michelle on LinkedIn:
https://au/linkedin.com/in/michellegibbings

Email Michelle at:
michelle@michellegibbings.com

References

1. Davenport, T. and Beck, J.C. (2002). "The strategy and structure of firms in the attention economy", http://iveybusinessjournal.com/publication/the-strategy-and-structure-of-firms-in-the-attention-economy/, accessed 16 June 2015.
2. Dweck, C. (2012), *Mindset: How you can fulfil your potential*, New York, Random House.
3. Schwartz, D.J. (1959), *The Magic of Thinking Big*, New York, Simon and Schuster.
4. Covey, S. (1989), *The 7 Habits of Highly Effective People*, New York, Simon and Schuster.
5. Mandela, N. (1995), *The Long Walk to Freedom*, London, Abacus.
6. Kabat-Zinn, J. (2015), http://www.mindful.org/jon-kabat-zinn-video-series-on-mindful-org/, accessed on 5 October 2015.
7. Lipton, B. (2005), *The Biology of Belief*, Alexandria, Hay House, p. 118.
8. Lipton, B. (2005), *The Biology of Belief*, Alexandria, Hay House, pp. 120-121.
9. Lyubomirsky, S., Sheldon, K. and Schkade, D. (2005), "Pursuing Happiness the architecture of sustainable change" *Review of General Psychology*, Vol 9, No 2, pp. 111-131.
10. Lyubomirsky, S., King, L. and Diener, E. (2005), "The benefits of positive affect: does happiness lead to success?" *Psychological Bulletin*, Vol 131, No. 6, pp. 803-855.
11. Ariely, D. (2012), "Why we lie", *Wall Street Journal*, 26 May 2012, http://www.wsj.com/news/articles/SB10001424052702304840904577422090013997320?mod=wsj_share_tweet&mg=reno64-wsj&url=http%3A%2F%2Fonline.wsj.com%2Farticle%2FSB10001424052702304840904577422090013997320.html%3Fmod%3Dwsj_share_tweet

12. Kranhold, K., Lee, B. and Benson, M. (2012), "New Documents Show Enron Traders Manipulated California Energy Costs", *Wall Street Journal*, 7 May 2012, http://www.wsj.com/articles/SB10207186373822744 00

13. Time (2007), "The worst cars of all time", *Time*, http://content.time.com/time/specials/2007/article/0,28804,1658545_1658498_1657866,00.html

14. Festinger, L. (1957), *A theory of cognitive dissonance*, Stanford, Stanford University Press.

15. Brenner, M. (1996), "The man who knew too much", *Vanity Fair*, May 1996, http://www.vanityfair.com/magazine/1996/05/wigand199605

16. Salter, C. (2002), "Jeffrey Wigand: The whistle blower", *Fast Company*, 30 April 2002 http://www.fastcompany.com/65027/jeffrey-wigand-whistle-blower

17. Chabris, C. and Simons, D. (2010), *The Invisible Gorilla*, New York, Crown Publishers.

18. Kahneman, D. (2011), *Thinking fast and slow*, New York, Farrar, Straus and Giroux.

19. Banaji, M., Bazerman, M. and Chugh, D. (2003), "How unethical are you?" *Harvard Business Review*, December 2003, p. 59.

20. George, B. (2007), *True North: Discover your authentic leadership*, San Francisco, Jossey-Bass.

21. Bigelow, K. (unknown), Quote, http://www.brainyquote.com/quotes/quotes/k/kathrynbig254781.html

22. Cleary, T. (2004), *Zen Lessons: the art of leadership*, Boston, Shambhala, p. 201.

23. Soll, J., Milkman, K. and Payne, J. (2015), "Outsmart your own biases" *Harvard Business Review*, May 2015. p. 68.

24. The Economist, (2009), "Guru: Alfred Sloan", http://www.economist.com/node/13047099, 30 January 2009.

25. Peck, M., Scott. (1978). *The Road Less Travelled: A new psychology for love, traditional values, and spiritual growth*. Simon & Schuster, New York, pp. 15.

26. Bossidy, L. and Charan, R. (2011), *Execution: The discipline of getting things done,* London, Random House, p. 89.
27. Gardner, D. (2011). *Future Babble: Why pundits are hedgehogs and foxes know best,* New York, Penguin, p. 134.
28. Rock, D. (2009), *Your brain at work,* New York, Harper Collins, p. 33.
29. Schwartz, T. and McCarthy, C. (2007), "Manage your energy not your time", *Harvard Business Review,* October 2007.
30. Kanter, R. M. (2010), "Seven Truths to live change by", *Harvard Business Review,* 23 August 2010.
31. Anders Ericsson, K., Krampe, R. and Tesch-Romer, C. (1993), "The Role of Deliberate Practice in the Acquisition of Expert Performance", *Psychological Review* Vol. 100. No. 3, pp. 363-406
32. Welch, J. (2000), Letter to GE shareholders, http://www.ge.com/annual00/letter/page4.html, accessed 5 October 2015.
33. Heifetz, R., Grashow, A. and Linsky M. (2009), *The Practice of Adaptive Leadership,* Boston, Harvard Business Press.
34. Bridges, W. (1995), *Managing Transitions,* London, Nicholas Brealey Publishing.
35. Anand, N. and Barsoux, J.L. (2014), *Quest: Leading Global Transformations,* Lausanne, International Institute for Management Development, p. 211.
36. Schein, E. (1999), *The Corporate Culture Survival Guide,* San Francisco, Jossey-Bass, p. 27.
37. Sapolsky, R.M. (2007), "Peace among primates", *The Greater Good,* 1 September 2007, www.greatergood.berkeley.edu/article/item/peace_among_primates, accessed 4 May 2015
38. Robbins, S.P., Waters-Marsh, T, et al (1994), *Organisational Behavioiur: concepts, controversies and applications,* Sydney, Prentice Hall, p. 522.
39. Gladwell, M. (2001), *The Tipping Point: How little things can make a big difference,* New York, Little, Brown & Company.
40. Burton, L., Weston, D. and Kowalski, R. (2009), *Psychology,* 2nd Ed, Milton, John Wiley and Sons.

41. Deci, E. (1971), "Effects of externally mediated rewards on intrinsic motivation" *Journal of Personality and Social Psychology*, Vol. 18, No. 1 pp. 105-115.

42. Pimental, B. (2007), "Jeffrey Pfeffer: How Employee Financial Incentives Can Backfire", *Insights by Stanford Business*, http://www.gsb.stanford.edu/insights/jeffrey-pfeffer-how-employee-financial-incentives-can-backfire, 1 September 2007.

43. Ariely, D. (2008), "What's the value of a big bonus", Blog, http://danariely.com/2008/11/20/what%E2%80%99s-the-value-of-a-big-bonus/

44. Furnham, A. and Taylor, J. (2011), *Bad Apples: Identify, prevent and manage negative behaviour at work,* Hampshire, Palgrave Macmillan, p. 53.

45. Amabile, T. and Kramer, S.J. (2010), "What really motivates workers", *Harvard Business Review,* https://hbr.org/2010/01/the-hbr-list-breakthrough-ideas-for-2010/ar/1

46. Csikszentimahalyi. M. (2008), *Flow: The Psychology of Optimal Experience,* New York, Harper Collins.

47. Rock, D. (2008), "SCARF: a brain based model for collaborating with and influencing others" *Neuroleadership Journal.* No. 1.

48. Kegan, R. and Lahey, L. (2001), *How the way we talk can change the way we work,* San Francisco, Jossey-Bass, p. 63.

49. Verplanken, B. and Wood, W. (2006), "Interventions to break and create consumer habits" *Journal of Public Policy and Marketing,* Vol. 25 (1) Spring 2006, pp. 90-103.

50. Hopkins, A. (2005), *Safety, Culture and Risk: The Organisational Causes of Disasters,* Sydney, CCH Australia.

51. Spaulding, T. (2010), *It's not just who you know,* New York, Broadway Books, p. 46.

52. Carnegie, D. (1964), *How to win friends and influence people,* New York, Simon and Schuster.

53. Spaulding, T. (2010), *It's not just who you know,* New York, Broadway Books, p. 226.

54. Cialdini, R. (1984), Influence: *The Psychology of Persuasion*, New York, Harper Collins, p. 17-18.
55. Naftulin, D. H., Ware, J.E. and Donnelly, F. A. (1973), "The Doctor Fox lecture: a paradigm of educational seduction", *Journal of Medical Education*, Vol. 48, July 1973, pp. 630-635.
56. Gardner, D. (2011). *Future Babble: Why pundits are hedgehogs and foxes know best*, New York, Penguin, p. 150.
57. Dweck, C. (2012), *Mindset: How you can fulfil your potential*, New York, Random House, p. 139.
58. Ury, W. (2007), *The power of a positive no: how to say no and still get to yes*, London, Hodder & Stoughton, p. 217.
59. Block, P. (2011), *Flawless Consulting*, San Francisco, Pfeiffer, p. 65.

Index

Adler, Alfred 167
agile productivity 79, 82
amygdala 25, 43, 44, 75, 150
anchoring 64-65
Argyris 55
Ariely, Dan 54, 144
Artistotle 47
Aurelius, Marcus 37

Ball, Lucille 92
Battista, Orlando A. 72
Bay of Pigs invasion 66
behaviour 138, 141, 161
bias 54, 60-67, 75, 78, 133
Bigelow, Kathryn 69
Block, Peter 206
Bossidy, Larry 82
brain, 64, 98-104
Branson, Richard 188
Bridges, William 115
Buddha 53

Carnegie, Dale 169
Castro, Fidel 66
Chabris, Christopher 60
change 27-29, 33, 76, 96-99, 110-117, 121, 125-133, 137, 149, 152, 157-158, 162-163, 176
change, organisational 114, 190
Charan, Ram 82
Charles, Ray 92
Churchill, Winston 137

Cialdini, Robert 170
Circle of Concern 40, 134
Circle of Influence 40, 134
cognitive dissonance 58
comfort zone 28-29, 33, 98
communication 183-186, 190, 193, 210
competitive advantage 4
compliance 1-2
consciousness 28-30, 57, 70
control 88
Covey, Stephen 40, 134
Csikszentimahalyi, Mihaly 148
culture 11, 54, 110, 117-120, 134, 135

Darwin, Charles 92
Deci, Edward 144-145
decision-making 11, 54, 61-63, 66-67, 75, 80-88, 117, 135, 149, 164
Dweck, Carol 20, 199

efficiency 79
Emerson, Ralph Waldo 160
Enron 55
environment 11, 54-56, 69, 80, 117
ethical 54, 56, 69

feedback 21, 79, 111, 149
Festinger, Leon 58

'fight or flight' 25, 44, 75, 200
focus 12, 100
Ford Pinto 56
'fundamental attribution error' 22
frameworks 9
Frankl, Viktor 34
French, John 122

Gardner, Dan 89, 182
Gardner, Howard 99
George, Bill 68, 153
Gladwell, Malcolm 126
goals 51, 95

habits 160-162
happiness 47-52, 167-168
Herzberg, Frederick 141
hierarchy 8, 76
Hopkins, Professor Andrew 163
Hosseini, Khaled 72
Huxley, Aldous 19

Implicit Association test 65
influence, ladder of 6, 9-10
influence, positions of 7
inner voice 24-26, 47, 98

Kahneman, Daniel 64, 181
Kanter, Professor Rosabeth Moss 94, 140
Kegan, Robert 154
Keller, Helen 39
Kennedy, John F. 66
Kummer, Hans 118

Lahey, Lisa 154
Lao-tzu 152, 198
leadership 6, 22-23, 79, 113, 116, 119-123, 136-138, 142-143, 147, 152-157, 163-164, 166, 184

Lincoln, Abraham 189
Lipton, Dr Bruce 44

managers, entry level 9
Mandela, Nelson 41
Marlowe, Christopher 58
Maslow, Abraham 141
McClelland, David 141
meditation 39, 42, 46, 50
memory 100-102
Menuhin, Yehudi 95
meta-cognition 70
mindfulness 39, 42-46
mindset 6, 11-15, 20, 26-35, 40, 52, 75, 96, 150
mindset, empowered 35
motivation 142, 145-149

Napoleon 36
negotiation 12, 183, 194, 196-201, 205-206, 210
neurology 74
Nobel Prize 5

Obama, Barack 85
optimism 41

Peck, M. Scott 81
Perry, William 60
Pfeffer, Jeffrey 144
Phelps, Michael 102
philosophy 74
physiology 74
Picasso, Pablo 79
planning, strategic 81
Pollock, Jackson 92-93
Porter, Michael 4
power 8, 122-123
practice 101
Presley, Elvis 92

productivity 91, 150
Professor Black 151
Proust, Marcel 92
psychology 74

Rath, Tom 168
Raven, Bertram 122
relationship-building 170
relationships 139, 153, 167, 169-175, 178, 197-199, 210
relationships, insight-based 139-140
reputation 53
reputation, professional 59
resilience 36-38, 93, 98
risk 1-2, 130
Rock, David 90, 150
Rockefeller, John D. III 112

Schein, Edgar 117
Schon 55
Schwartz, David 33
Seneca 209
Senge, Peter 109

Shakespeare, William 27
Simon, Herbert 5
Simons, Dan 60
sleep 100, 102
Sloan, Alfred 78
social psychologists 65
social responsibility 13
Spaulding, Tom 169
stakeholders 12, 172, 174, 177-179
Strayed, Cheryl 69
stress 43-46
Sullivan, Anne 40

team 131, 135-136, 143, 158, 162-164, 166
technical roles 2
trigger 45, 67-68, 70, 155, 158-159

Ury, William 201

values 55
Verplanken, Bas 161

Wigand, Jeffrey 59
Wood, Wendy 161

Printed by Libri Plureos GmbH in Hamburg, Germany